EinFach Englisch

Classic and Contemporary American Short Stories

Edited by
Dennis Hannemann

Series Editor:
Hans Kröger

Sprachliche Betreuung: Michelle Ruth Kloppenburg

© 2018 Bildungshaus Schulbuchverlage Westermann Schroedel Diesterweg Schöningh Winklers GmbH, Georg-Westermann-Allee 66, 38104 Braunschweig
www.westermann.de

Das Werk und seine Teile sind urheberrechtlich geschützt. Jede Nutzung in anderen als den gesetzlich zugelassenen bzw. vertraglich zugestandenen Fällen bedarf der vorherigen schriftlichen Einwilligung des Verlages. Nähere Informationen zur vertraglich gestatteten Anzahl von Kopien finden Sie auf www.schulbuchkopie.de.

Für Verweise (Links) auf Internet-Adressen gilt folgender Haftungshinweis: Trotz sorgfältiger inhaltlicher Kontrolle wird die Haftung für die Inhalte der externen Seiten ausgeschlossen. Für den Inhalt dieser externen Seiten sind ausschließlich deren Betreiber verantwortlich. Sollten Sie daher auf kostenpflichtige, illegale oder anstößige Inhalte treffen, so bedauern wir dies ausdrücklich und bitten Sie, uns umgehend per E-Mail davon in Kenntnis zu setzen, damit beim Nachdruck der Verweis gelöscht wird.

Druck A^5 / Jahr 2024
Alle Drucke der Serie A sind im Unterricht parallel verwendbar.

Umschlagfoto: Harry Horton/Alamy Stock Foto
Druck und Bindung: Westermann Druck GmbH, Georg-Westermann-Allee 66, 38104 Braunschweig

ISBN 978-3-14-**041290**-2

Contents

Getting started 4

Texts

Dreams and realities
- Ernest Hemingway: "A Clean, Well-Lighted Place" 6
- F. Scott Fitzgerald: "Babylon Revisited" 10
- Langston Hughes: "One Friday Morning" 29

Multi-ethnic America
- Leslie Marmon Silko: "Tony's Story" 37
- Jhumpa Lahiri: "Sexy" 43
- Junot Díaz: "Nilda" 63

Global perspectives
- Deborah Eisenberg: "Twilight of the Superheroes" 71
- Charles Baxter: "Charity" 98
- Joan Silber: "About My Aunt" 111

Con-Texts

- About the authors 127
- This collection 133
- Maps 135
- The American short story: Introduction to the genre and historical overview 137
- Quotations from authors 139

Developing skills 141

Acknowledgements 146

Getting started

Richard Estes, *Columbus Circle Subway Station*, oil on board, 2012

Richard Estes, *Water Taxi, Mount Desert*, oil on canvas, 1999

To get started, choose one of the two assignments:

1. a) Describe the images. Take into account the location, figures, composition, contrasts and atmosphere.
   b) Based on your experience of reading German or English short stories, explain why each painting could be matched to a short story.

2. Take the role of an author. Choose one painting and use it as a source of inspiration for the next short story you are going to write. Jot down ideas with regard to characters, setting and plot. Then, write the first few sentences of your short story. They should catch the reader's attention.

A Clean, Well-Lighted Place
Ernest Hemingway

It was late and everyone had left the café except an old man who sat in the shadow the leaves of the tree made against the electric light. In the daytime the street was dusty, but at night the dew settled the dust and the old man liked to sit late because he was deaf and now at night it was quiet and he felt the difference. The two waiters inside the cafe knew that the old man was a little drunk, and while he was a good client they knew that if he became too drunk he would leave without paying, so they kept watch on him.

"Last week he tried to commit suicide," one waiter said.

"Why?"

"He was in despair."

"What about?"

"Nothing."

"How do you know it was nothing?"

"He has plenty of money."

They sat together at a table that was close against the wall near the door of the café and looked at the terrace where the tables were all empty except where the old man sat in the shadow of the leaves of the tree that moved slightly in the wind. A girl and a soldier went by in the street. The street light shone on the brass number on his collar. The girl wore no head covering and hurried beside him.

"The guard will pick him up," one waiter said.

"What does it matter if he gets what he's after?"

"He had better get off the street now. The guard will get him. They went by five minutes ago."

The old man sitting in the shadow rapped on his saucer with his glass. The younger waiter went over to him.

"What do you want?"

The old man looked at him. "Another brandy," he said.

"You'll be drunk," the waiter said. The old man looked at him. The waiter went away.

"He'll stay all night," he said to his colleague. "I'm sleepy now. I never get to bed before three o'clock. He should have killed himself last week."

The waiter took the brandy bottle and another saucer from

---

dew *Tau*

collar *Kragen*

★ **saucer** a small dish that you put a tea cup or coffee cup on

Why is the younger waiter upset?

the counter inside the café and marched out to the old man's table. He put down the saucer and poured the glass full of brandy.

"You should have killed yourself last week," he said to the deaf man.

The old man motioned with his finger. "A little more," he said. The waiter poured on into the glass so that the brandy slopped over and ran down the stem into the top saucer of the pile.

"Thank you," the old man said. The waiter took the bottle back inside the café. He sat down at the table with his colleague again.

"He's drunk now," he said.

"He's drunk every night."

"What did he want to kill himself for?"

"How should I know?"

"How did he do it?"

"He hung himself with a rope."

"Who cut him down?"

"His niece."

"Why did they do it?"

"Fear for his soul."

"How much money has he got?"

"He's got plenty."

"He must be eighty years old."

"Anyway I should say he was eighty."

"I wish he would go home. I never get to bed before three o'clock. What kind of hour is that to go to bed?"

"He stays up because he likes it."

"He's lonely. I'm not lonely. I have a wife waiting in bed for me."

"He had a wife once too."

"A wife would be no good to him now."

"You can't tell. He might be better with a wife."

"His niece looks after him."

"I know. You said she cut him down."

"I wouldn't want to be that old. An old man is a nasty thing."

"Not always. This old man is clean. He drinks without spilling. Even now, drunk. Look at him."

"I don't want to look at him. I wish he would go home. He has no regard for those who must work."

The old man looked from his glass across the square, then over at the waiters.

"Another brandy," he said, pointing to his glass. The waiter who was in a hurry came over.

"Finished," he said, speaking with that omission of syntax stu-

to pour full to fill a cup or glass with a drink

omission of syntax here: incomplete sentences

pid people employ when talking to drunken people or foreigners. "No more tonight. Close now."

"Another," said the old man.

"No. Finished." The waiter wiped the edge of the table with a towel and shook his head.

The old man stood up, slowly counted the saucers, took a leather coin purse from his pocket and paid for the drinks, leaving half a peseta tip.

The waiter watched him go down the street, a very old man walking unsteadily but with dignity.

"Why didn't you let him stay and drink?" the unhurried waiter asked. They were putting up the shutters. "It is not half past two."

"I want to go home to bed."

"What is an hour?"

"More to me than to him."

"An hour is the same."

"You talk like an old man yourself. He can buy a bottle and drink at home."

"It's not the same."

"No, it is not," agreed the waiter with a wife. He did not wish to be unjust. He was only in a hurry.

"And you? You have no fear of going home before your usual hour?"

"Are you trying to insult me?"

"No, hombre, only to make a joke."

"No," the waiter who was in a hurry said, rising from pulling down the metal shutters. "I have confidence. I am all confidence."

"You have youth, confidence, and a job," the older waiter said. "You have everything."

"And what do you lack?"

"Everything but work."

"You have everything I have."

"No. I have never had confidence and I am not young."

"Come on. Stop talking nonsense and lock up."

"I am of those who like to stay late at the café," the older waiter said. "With all those who do not want to go to bed. With all those who need a light for the night."

"I want to go home and into bed."

"We are of two different kinds," the older waiter said. He was dressed now to go home. "It is not only a question of youth and confidence, although those things are very beautiful. Each night I am reluctant to close up because there may be someone who needs the café."

"Hombre, there are bodegas open all night long."

"You do not understand. This is a clean and pleasant café. It is well lighted. The light is very good and also, now, there are shadows of leaves."

"Good-night," said the younger waiter.

"Good-night," the other said. Turning off the electric light he continued the conversation with himself. It is the light of course but it is necessary that the place be clean and pleasant. You do not want music. Certainly you do not want music. Nor can you stand before a bar with dignity although that is all that is provided for these hours. What did he fear? It was not fear or dread. It was a nothing that he knew too well. It was all a nothing and a man was nothing too. It was only that and light was all it needed and a certain cleanness and order. Some lived in it and never felt it but he knew it all was nada y pues nada y nada y pues nada. Our nada who art in nada, nada be thy name thy kingdom nada thy will be nada in nada as it is in nada. Give us this nada our daily nada and nada us our nada as we nada our nadas and nada us not into nada but deliver us from nada; pues nada. Hail nothing full of nothing, nothing is with thee. He smiled and stood before a bar with a shining steam pressure coffee machine.

"What's yours?" asked the barman.

"Nada."

"Otro loco mas," said the barman and turned away.

"A little cup," said the waiter.

The barman poured it for him.

"The light is very bright and pleasant but the bar is unpolished," the waiter said.

The barman looked at him but did not answer. It was too late at night for conversation.

"You want another copita?" the barman asked.

"No, thank you," said the waiter and went out. He disliked bars and bodegas. A clean, well-lighted café was a very different thing. Now, without thinking further, he would go home to his room. He would lie in the bed and finally, with daylight, he would go to sleep. After all, he said to himself, it is probably only insomnia. Many must have it.

Ernest Hemingway, Winner Take Nothing, London: Arrow Books, 2006 (1994), pp. 55–59.

---

bodega (Sp.) wine bar

The **Lord's Prayer** (or **Our Father**):
Our Father who art in heaven, hallowed be thy name. Thy kingdom come. Thy will be done in earth, as it is in heaven. Give us this day our daily bread. And forgive us our debts, as we forgive our debtors. And lead us not into temptation, but deliver us from evil: For thine is the kingdom, and the power, and the glory, for ever. Amen.
(Matthew 6: 9–13; King James Version)

nada (Sp.) nothing
y pues (Sp.) and then

thy (old) your
thee (old) you

otro loco mas (Sp.) another crazy guy

copita (Sp.) small glass

***insomnia** a condition in which you have difficulty sleeping

Babylon Revisited
F. Scott Fitzgerald

I

"And where's Mr. Campbell?" Charlie asked.

Gone to Switzerland. Mr. Campbell's a pretty sick man, Mr. Wales."

"I'm sorry to hear that. And George Hardt?" Charlie inquired.

"Back in America, gone to work."

"And where is the Snow Bird?"

"He was in here last week. Anyway, his friend, Mr. Schaeffer, is in Paris."

Two familiar names from the long list of a year and a half ago. Charlie scribbled an address in his notebook and tore out the page.

"If you see Mr. Schaeffer, give him this," he said. "It's my brother-in-law's address. I haven't settled on a hotel yet."

He was not really disappointed to find Paris was so empty. But the stillness in the Ritz bar was strange and portentous. It was not an American bar any more — he felt polite in it, and not as if he owned it. It had gone back into France. He felt the stillness from the moment he got out of the taxi and saw the doorman, usually in a frenzy of activity at this hour, gossiping with a *chasseur* by the servants' entrance.

Passing through the corridor, he heard only a single, bored voice in the once-clamorous women's room. When he turned into the bar he traveled the twenty feet of green carpet with his eyes fixed straight ahead by old habit; and then, with his foot firmly on the rail, he turned and surveyed the room, encountering only a single pair of eyes that fluttered up from a newspaper in the corner. Charlie asked for the head barman, Paul, who in the latter days of the bull market had come to work in his own custom-built car — disembarking, however, with due nicety at the nearest corner. But Paul was at his country house today and Alix giving him information.

"No, no more," Charlie said, "I'm going slow these days."

Alix congratulated him: "You were going pretty strong a couple of years ago."

"I'll stick to it all right," Charlie assured him. "I've stuck to it for over a year and a half now."

"How do you find conditions in America?"

"I haven't been to America for months. I'm in business in Prague, representing a couple of concerns there. They don't know about me down there."

Babylon
Babylon was a major city in ancient Mesopotamia, thriving between 1800 and 300 BC. In the Bible and in other ancient sources Babylon came to be associated with materialism, luxury, hubris and sensual pleasures.

portentous giving a warning about the future, *unheilvoll*

chasseur (Fr.) person who delivers messages

clamorous very noisy

to disembark to get off a ship or plane

What does the reader learn of Charlie's past?

Alix smiled.

"Remember the night of George Hardt's bachelor dinner here?" said Charlie, "By the way, what's become of Claude Fessenden?"

Alix lowered his voice confidentially: "He's in Paris, but he doesn't come here any more. Paul doesn't allow it. He ran up a bill of thirty thousand francs, charging all his drinks and his lunches, and usually his dinner, for more than a year. And when Paul finally told him he had to pay, he gave him a bad check."

Alix shook his head sadly.

"I don't understand it, such a dandy fellow. Now he's all bloated up –" He made a plump apple of his hands.

Charlie watched a group of strident queens installing themselves in a corner.

"Nothing affects them," he thought. "Stocks rise and fall, people loaf or work, but they go on forever." The place oppressed him. He called for the dice and shook with Alix for the drink.

"Here for long, Mr. Wales?"

"I'm here for four or five days to see my little girl."

"Oh-h! You have a little girl?"

Outside, the fire-red, gas-blue, ghost-green signs shone smokily through the tranquil rain. It was late afternoon and the streets were in movement; the *bistros* gleamed. At the corner of the Boulevard des Capucines he took a taxi. The Place de la Concorde moved by in pink majesty; they crossed the logical Seine, and Charlie felt the sudden provincial quality of the left bank.

Charlie directed his taxi to the Avenue de l'Opera, which was out of his way. But he wanted to see the blue hour spread over the magnificent façade, and imagine that the cab horns, playing endlessly the first few bars of *La Plus que Lent*, were the trumpets of the Second Empire. They were closing the iron grill in front of Brentano's Book-store, and people were already at dinner behind the trim little bourgeois hedge of Duval's. He had never eaten at a really cheap restaurant in Paris. Five-course dinner, four francs fifty, eighteen cents, wine included. For some odd reason he wished that he had.

As they rolled on to the Left Bank and he felt its sudden provincialism, he thought, "I spoiled this city for myself. I didn't realize it, but the days came along one after another, and then two years were gone, and everything was gone, and I was gone."

He was thirty-five, and good to look at. The Irish mobility of his face was sobered by a deep wrinkle between his eyes. As

---

bachelor *Junggeselle*

bloated up *aufgedunsen*

strident with an unpleasantly harsh voice

★ **stocks** (pl.) *Aktien*

to oppress here: to make sb feel depressed and uncomfortable

loaf to be lazy

Left Bank
The Left Bank (Rive Gauche) is the southern part of Paris, divided by the River Seine. It has often been linked with intellectual life, in particular during the 1920s, when artists and writers like Hemingway and Fitzgerald resided there. The Sorbonne and the Latin Quarter are located on the Left Bank.

La plus que lente piano composition by French composer Claude Debussy (1862–1918)

wrinkle *Falte*

he rang his brother-in-law's bell in the Rue Palatine, the wrinkle deepened till it pulled down his brows; he felt a cramping sensation in his belly. From behind the maid who opened the door darted a lovely little girl of nine who shrieked "Daddy!" and flew up, struggling like a fish, into his arms. She pulled his head around by one ear and set her cheek against his.
"My old pie," he said.
"Oh, daddy, daddy, daddy, daddy, dads, dads, dads!"
She drew him into the salon, where the family waited, a boy and a girl his daughter's age, his sister-in-law and her husband. He greeted Marion with his voice pitched carefully to avoid either feigned enthusiasm or dislike, but her response was more frankly tepid, though she minimized her expression of unalterable distrust by directing her regard toward his child. The two men clasped hands in a friendly way and Lincoln Peters rested his for a moment on Charlie's shoulder.

The room was warm and comfortably American. The three children moved intimately about, playing through the yellow oblongs that led to other rooms; the cheer of six o'clock spoke in the eager smacks of the fire and the sounds of French activity in the kitchen. But Charlie did not relax; his heart sat up rigidly in his body and he drew confidence from his daughter, who from time to time came close to him, holding in her arms the doll he had brought.

"Really extremely well," he declared in answer to Lincoln's question. "There's a lot of business there that isn't moving at all, but we're doing even better than ever. In fact, damn well. I'm bringing my sister over from America next month to keep house for me. My income last year was bigger than it was when I had money. You see, the Czechs —"

His boasting was for a specific purpose; but after a moment, seeing a faint restiveness in Lincoln's eye, he changed the subject:

"Those are fine children of yours, well brought up, good manners."

"We think Honoria's a great little girl too."

Marion Peters came back from the kitchen. She was a tall woman with worried eyes, who had once possessed a fresh American loveliness. Charlie had never been sensitive to it and was always surprised when people spoke of how pretty she had been. From the first there had been an instinctive antipathy between them.

"Well, how do you find Honoria?" she asked.

"Wonderful. I was astonished how much she's grown in ten months. All the children are looking well."

"We haven't had a doctor for a year. How do you like being back in Paris?"

"It seems very funny to see so few Americans around."

"I'm delighted," Marion said vehemently. "Now at least you can go into a store without their assuming you're a millionaire. We've suffered like everybody, but on the whole it's a good deal pleasanter."

"But it was nice while it lasted," Charlie said. "We were a sort of royalty, almost infallible, with a sort of magic around us. In the bar this afternoon" — he stumbled, seeing his mistake — "there wasn't a man I knew."

She looked at him keenly. "I should think you'd have had enough of bars."

"I only stayed a minute. I take one drink every afternoon, and no more."

"Don't you want a cocktail before dinner?" Lincoln asked.

"I take only one drink every afternoon, and I've had that."

"I hope you keep to it," said Marion.

Her dislike was evident in the coldness with which she spoke, but Charlie only smiled; he had larger plans. Her very aggressiveness gave him an advantage, and he knew enough to wait. He wanted them to initiate the discussion of what they knew had brought him to Paris.

At dinner he couldn't decide whether Honoria was most like him or her mother. Fortunate if she didn't combine the traits of both that had brought them to disaster. A great wave of protectiveness went over him. He thought he knew what to do for her. He believed in character; he wanted to jump back a whole generation and trust in character again as the eternally valuable element. Everything else wore out.

He left soon after dinner, but not to go home. He was curious to see Paris by night with clearer and more judicious eyes than those of other days. He bought a *strapontin* for the Casino and watched Josephine Baker go through her chocolate arabesques.

After an hour he left and strolled toward Montmartre, up the Rue Pigalle into the Place Blanche. The rain had stopped and there were a few people in evening clothes disembarking from taxis in front of cabarets, and *cocottes* prowling singly or in pairs, and many Negroes. He passed a lighted door from which issued music, and stopped with the sense of familiarity; it was Bricktop's, where he had parted with so many hours and so much money. A few doors farther on he found another ancient rendezvous and incautiously put his head inside. Immediately an eager orchestra burst into sound, a pair of profes-

---

infallible not capable of making mistakes

* to wear out *(sich) abnutzen*

strapontin (Fr.) inexpensive seat
Josephine Baker (1906–1975), an American-born French singer, dancer, and actress
arabesque piece of music of oriental character

cocotte (Fr.) prostitute

sional dancers leaped to their feet and a maître d'hôtel swooped toward him, crying, "Crowd just arriving, sir!" But he withdrew quickly.

"You have to be damn drunk," he thought.

Zelli's was closed, the bleak and sinister cheap hotels surrounding it were dark; up in the Rue Blanche there was more light and a local, colloquial French crowd. The Poet's Cave had disappeared, but the two great mouths of the Café of Heaven and the Café of Hell still yawned — even devoured, as he watched, the meager contents of a tourist bus — a German, a Japanese, and an American couple who glanced at him with frightened eyes.

So much for the effort and ingenuity of Montmartre. All the catering to vice and waste was on an utterly childish scale, and he suddenly realized the meaning of the word "dissipate" — to dissipate into thin air; to make nothing out of something. In the little hours of the night every move from place to place was an enormous human jump, an increase of paying for the privilege of slower and slower motion.

He remembered thousand-franc notes given to an orchestra for playing a single number, hundred-franc notes tossed to a doorman for calling a cab.

But it hadn't been given for nothing.

It had been given, even the most wildly squandered sum, as an offering to destiny that he might not remember the things most worth remembering, the things that now he would always remember — his child taken from his control, his wife escaped to a grave in Vermont.

In the glare of a *brasserie* a woman spoke to him. He bought her some eggs and coffee, and then, eluding her encouraging stare, gave her a twenty-franc note and took a taxi to his hotel.

II

He woke upon a fine fall day — football weather. The depression of yesterday was gone and he liked the people on the streets. At noon he sat opposite Honoria at Le Grand Vatel, the only restaurant he could think of not reminiscent of champagne dinners and long luncheons that began at two and ended in a blurred and vague twilight.

"Now, how about vegetables? Oughtn't you to have some vegetables?"

"Well, yes."

"Here's *épinards* and *chou-fleur* and carrots and *haricots*."

"I'd like *chou-fleur*."

"Wouldn't you like to have two vegetables?"

"I usually only have one at lunch."

The waiter was pretending to be inordinately fond of children. *"Qu'elle est mignonne la petite! Elle parle exactement comme une Française."*

"How about dessert? Shall we wait and see?"

The waiter disappeared. Honoria looked at her father expectantly.

"What are we going to do?"

"First, we're going to that toy store in the Rue Saint-Honoré and buy you anything you like. And then we're going to the vaudeville at the Empire."

She hesitated. "I like it about the vaudeville, but not the toy store."

"Why not?"

"Well, you brought me this doll." She had it with her. "And I've got lots of things. And we're not rich any more, are we?"

"We never were. But today you are to have anything you want."

"All right," she agreed resignedly.

When there had been her mother and a French nurse he had been inclined to be strict; now he extended himself, reached out for a new tolerance; he must be both parents to her and not shut any of her out of communication.

"I want to get to know you," he said gravely. "First let me introduce myself. My name is Charles J. Wales, of Prague."

"Oh, daddy!" her voice cracked with laughter.

"And who are you, please?" he persisted, and she accepted a role immediately: "Honoria Wales, Rue Palatine, Paris."

"Married or single?"

"No, not married. Single."

He indicated the doll. "But I see you have a child, madame."

Unwilling to disinherit it, she took it to her heart and thought quickly: "Yes, I've been married, but I'm not married now. My husband is dead."

He went on quickly, "And the child's name?"

"Simone. That's after my best friend at school."

"I'm very pleased that you're doing so well at school."

"I'm third this month," she boasted. "Elsie" — that was her cousin — "is only about eighteenth, and Richard is about at the bottom."

"You like Richard and Elsie, don't you?"

"Oh, yes. I like Richard quite well and I like her all right."

Cautiously and casually he asked: "And Aunt Marion and Uncle Lincoln — which do you like best?"

"Oh, Uncle Lincoln, I guess."

Qu'elle ... (Fr.) How cute she is! She speaks exactly like a French girl.

vaudeville (old) theatre hosting various kinds of entertainment

He was increasingly aware of her presence. As they came in, a murmur of "... adorable" followed them, and now the people at the next table bent all their silences upon her, staring as if she were something no more conscious than a flower.

"Why don't I live with you?" she asked suddenly. "Because mamma's dead?"

"You must stay here and learn more French. It would have been hard for daddy to take care of you so well."

"I don't really need much taking care of any more. I do everything for myself."

Going out of the restaurant, a man and a woman unexpectedly hailed him.

"Well, the old Wales!"

"Hello there, Lorraine. ... Dunc."

Sudden ghosts out of the past: Duncan Schaeffer, a friend from college. Lorraine Quarries, a lovely, pale blonde of thirty; one of a crowd who had helped them make months into days in the lavish times of three years ago.

"My husband couldn't come this year," she said, in answer to his question, "We're poor as hell. So he gave me two hundred a month and told me I could do my worst on that. ... This your little girl?"

"What about coming back and sitting down?" Duncan asked.

"Can't do it." He was glad for an excuse. As always, he felt Lorraine's passionate, provocative attraction, but his own rhythm was different now.

"Well, how about dinner?" she asked.

"I'm not free. Give me your address and let me call you."

"Charlie, I believe you're sober," she said judicially. "I honestly believe he's sober, Dunc. Pinch him and see if he's sober."

Charlie indicated Honoria with his head. They both laughed.

"What's your address?" said Duncan skeptically.

He hesitated, unwilling to give the name of his hotel.

"I'm not settled yet. I'd better call you. We're going to see the vaudeville at the Empire."

"There! That's what I want to do," Lorraine said. "I want to see some clowns and acrobats and jugglers. That's just what we'll do, Dunc."

"We've got to do an errand first," said Charlie. "Perhaps we'll see you there."

"All right, you snob. ... Good-by, beautiful little girl."

"Good-by."

Honoria bobbed politely.

Somehow, an unwelcome encounter. They liked him because he was functioning, because he was serious; they wanted to see him, because he was stronger than they were now, because they wanted to draw a certain sustenance from his strength.

sustenance here: support

At the Empire, Honoria proudly refused to sit upon her father's folded coat. She was already an individual with a code of her own, and Charlie was more and more absorbed by the desire of putting a little of himself into her before she crystallized utterly. It was hopeless to try to know her in so short a time.

utterly completely

Between the acts they came upon Duncan and Lorraine in the lobby where the band was playing.

"Have a drink?"

"All right, but not up at the bar. We'll take a table."

"The perfect father."

Listening abstractedly to Lorraine, Charlie watched Honoria's eyes leave their table, and he followed them wistfully about the room, wondering what they saw. He met her glance and she smiled.

wistfully wehmütig

"I liked that lemonade," she said.

What had she said? What had he expected? Going home in a taxi afterward, he pulled her over until her head rested against his chest.

"Darling, do you ever think about your mother?"

"Yes, sometimes," she answered vaguely.

"I don't want you to forget her. Have you got a picture of her?"

"Yes, I think so. Anyhow, Aunt Marion has. Why don't you want me to forget her?"

"She loved you very much."

"I loved her too."

They were silent for a moment,

"Daddy, I want to come and live with you," she said suddenly.

His heart leaped; he had wanted it to come like this.

"Aren't you perfectly happy?"

"Yes, but I love you better than anybody. And you love me better than anybody, don't you, now that mummy's dead?"

"Of course I do. But you won't always like me best, honey. You'll grow up and meet somebody your own age and go marry him and forget you ever had a daddy."

"Yes, that's true," she agreed tranquilly.

He didn't go in. He was coming back at nine o'clock and he wanted to keep himself fresh and new for the thing he must say then.

"When you're safe inside, just show yourself in that window."

"All right. Good-by, dads, dads, dads, dads."

He waited in the dark street until she appeared, all warm and glowing, in the window above and kissed her fingers out into the night.

III

They were waiting. Marion sat behind the coffee service in a dignified black dinner dress that just faintly suggested mourning. Lincoln was walking up and down with the animation of one who had already been talking. They were as anxious as he was to get into the question. He opened it almost immediately: "I suppose you know what I want to see you about — why I really came to Paris."

Marion played with the black stars on her necklace and frowned. "I'm awfully anxious to have a home," he continued. "And I'm awfully anxious to have Honoria in it. I appreciate your taking in Honoria for her mother's sake, but things have changed now" — he hesitated and then continued more forcibly – "changed radically with me, and I want to ask you to reconsider the matter. It would be silly for me to deny that about three years ago I was acting badly —"

Marion looked up at him with hard eyes.

"— but all that's over, As I told you, I haven't had more than a drink a day for over a year, and I take that drink deliberately, so that the idea of alcohol won't get too big in my imagination. You see the idea?"

"No," said Marion succinctly.

"It's a sort of stunt I set myself. It keeps the matter in proportion."

"I get you," said Lincoln. "You don't want to admit it's got any attraction for you."

"Something like that. Sometimes I forget and don't take it. But I try to take it. Anyhow, I couldn't afford to drink in my position. The people I represent are more than satisfied with what I've done, and I'm bringing my sister over from Burlington to keep house for me, and I want awfully to have Honoria too. You know that even when her mother and I weren't getting along well we never let anything that happened touch Honoria. I know she's fond of me and I know I'm able to take care of her and — well, there you are. How do you feel about it?"

He knew that now he would have to take a beating. It would last an hour or two hours, and it would be difficult, but if he modulated his inevitable resentment to the chastened attitude of the reformed sinner, he might win his point in the end.

Keep your temper, he told himself. You don't want to be justified. You want Honoria.

Lincoln spoke first: "We've been talking it over ever since we got your letter last month. We're happy to have Honoria here.

She's a dear little thing, and we're glad to be able to help her, but of course that isn't the question —"

Marion interrupted suddenly. "How long are you going to stay sober, Charlie?" she asked.

"Permanently, I hope."

"How can anybody count on that?"

"You know I never did drink heavily until I gave up business and came over here with nothing to do. Then Helen and I began to run around with —"

"Please leave Helen out of it. I can't bear to hear you talk about her like that."

He stared at her grimly; he had never been certain how fond of each other the sisters were in life.

"My drinking only lasted about a year and a half — from the time we came over until I — collapsed."

"It was time enough."

"It was time enough," he agreed.

"My duty is entirely to Helen," she said. "I try to think what she would have wanted me to do. Frankly, from the night you did that terrible thing you haven't really existed for me. I can't help that. She was my sister."

"Yes."

"When she was dying she asked me to look out for Honoria. If you hadn't been in a sanitarium then, it might have helped matters."

He had no answer.

"I'll never in my life be able to forget the morning when Helen knocked at my door, soaked to the skin and shivering and said you'd locked her out."

soaked wet, drenched

Charlie gripped the sides of the chair. This was more difficult than he expected; he wanted to launch out into a long expostulation and explanation, but he only said: "The night I locked her out —" and she interrupted, "I don't feel up to going over that again."

expostulation long explanation of strong disagreement

After a moment's silence Lincoln said: "We're getting off the subject. You want Marion to set aside her legal guardianship and give you Honoria. I think the main point for her is whether she has confidence in you or not."

"I don't blame Marion," Charlie said slowly, 'but I think she can have entire confidence in me. I had a good record up to three years ago. Of course, it's within human possibilities I might go wrong any time. But if we wait much longer I'll lose Honoria's childhood and my chance for a home." He shook his head, "I'll simply lose her, don't you see?"

"Yes, I see," said Lincoln.

"Why didn't you think of all this before?" Marion asked.
"I suppose I did, from time to time, but Helen and I were getting along badly. When I consented to the guardianship, I was flat on my back in a sanitarium and the market had cleaned me out. I knew I'd acted badly, and I thought if it would bring any peace to Helen, I'd agree to anything. But now it's different. I'm functioning, I'm behaving damn well, so far as —"
"Please don't swear at me," Marion said.

He looked at her, startled. With each remark the force of her dislike became more and more apparent. She had built up all her fear of life into one wall and faced it toward him. This trivial reproof was possibly the result of some trouble with the cook several hours before. Charlie became increasingly alarmed at leaving Honoria in this atmosphere of hostility against himself; sooner or later it would come out, in a word here, a shake of the head there, and some of that distrust would be irrevocably implanted in Honoria. But he pulled his temper down out of his face and shut it up inside him; he had won a point, for Lincoln realized the absurdity of Marion's remark and asked her lightly since when she had objected to the word "damn."

"Another thing," Charlie said: "I'm able to give her certain advantages now. I'm going to take a French governess to Prague with me. I've got a lease on a new apartment —"

He stopped, realizing that he was blundering. They couldn't be expected to accept with equanimity the fact that his income was again twice as large as their own.

"I suppose you can give her more luxuries than we can," said Marion. "When you were throwing away money we were living along watching every ten francs. ... I suppose you'll start doing it again."

"Oh, no," he said. "I've learned. I worked hard for ten years, you know until I got lucky in the market, like so many people. Terribly lucky. It won't happen again."

There was a long silence. All of them felt their nerves straining, and for the first time in a year Charlie wanted a drink. He was sure now that Lincoln Peters wanted him to have his child.

Marion shuddered suddenly; part of her saw that Charlie's feet were planted on the earth now, and her own maternal feeling recognized the naturalness of his desire; but she had lived for a long time with a prejudice — a prejudice founded on a curious disbelief in her sister's happiness, and which, in the shock of one terrible night, had turned to hatred for him. It had all happened at a point in her life where the discouragement of ill health and adverse circumstances made it neces-

---

startled surprised, alarmed

reproof criticism or blame

to blunder to make a clumsy mistake
equanimity calmness, self-control

to shudder to tremble

discouragement here: feeling of having lost hope

sary for her to believe in tangible villainy and a tangible villain.

"I can't help what I think!" she cried out suddenly. "How much you were responsible for Helen's death, I don't know. It's something you'll have to square with your own conscience."

An electric current of agony surged through him; for a moment he was almost on his feet, an unuttered sound echoing in his throat. He hung on to himself for a moment, another moment.

"Hold on there," said Lincoln uncomfortably. "I never thought you were responsible for that."

"Helen died of heart trouble," Charlie said dully.

"Yes, heart trouble." Marion spoke as if the phrase had another meaning for her.

Then, in the flatness that followed her outburst, she saw him plainly and she knew he had somehow arrived at control over the situation. Glancing at her husband, she found no help from him, and as abruptly as if it were a matter of no importance, she threw up the sponge.

"Do what you like!" she cried, springing up from her chair. "She's your child. I'm not the person to stand in your way. I think if it were my child I'd rather see her —" She managed to check herself. "You two decide it. I can't stand this. I'm sick. I'm going to bed."

She hurried from the room; after a moment Lincoln said: "This has been a hard day for her. You know how strongly she feels —" His voice was almost apologetic: "When a woman gets an idea in her head."

"Of course."

"It's going to be all right. I think she sees now that you — can provide for the child, and so we can't very well stand in your way or Honoria's way."

"Thank you, Lincoln."

"I'd better go along and see how she is."

"I'm going."

He was still trembling when he reached the street, but a walk down the Rue Bonaparte to the *quais* set him up, and as he crossed the Seine, fresh and new by the *quai* lamps, he felt exultant. But back in his room he couldn't sleep. The image of Helen haunted him. Helen whom he had loved so until they had senselessly begun to abuse each other's love, tear it into shreds. On that terrible February night that Marion remembered so vividly, a slow quarrel had gone on for hours. There was a scene at the Florida, and then he attempted to take her home, and then she kissed young Webb at a table; after that there was

tangible villainy concrete evil that can be felt

agony pain, torture

⬆ Why is Marion so upset?

apologetic saying sorry for doing sth wrong

quai (Fr.) river bank
exultant triumphant

★ **quarrel** disagreement

what she had hysterically said. When he arrived home alone he turned the key in the lock in wild anger. How could he know she would arrive an hour later alone, that there would be a snowstorm in which she wandered about in slippers, too confused to find a taxi? Then the aftermath, her escaping pneumonia by a miracle, and all the attendant horror. They were "reconciled," but that was the beginning of the end, and Marion, who had seen with her own eyes and who imagined it to be one of many scenes from her sister's martyrdom, never forgot.

Going over it again brought Helen nearer, and in the white, soft light that steals upon half sleep near morning he found himself talking to her again. She said that he was perfectly right about Honoria and that she wanted Honoria to be with him. She said she was glad he was being good and doing better. She said a lot of other things — very friendly things — but she was in a swing in a white dress, and swinging faster and faster all the time, so that at the end he could not hear clearly all that she said.

IV

He woke up feeling happy. The door of the world was open again. He made plans, vistas, futures for Honoria and himself, but suddenly he grew sad remembering all the plans he and Helen had made. She had not planned to die. The present was the thing — work to do and someone to love. But not to love too much, for he knew the injury that a father can do to a daughter or a mother to a son by attaching them too closely: afterward, out in the work, the child would seek in the marriage partner the same blind tenderness and, failing probably to find it, turn against love and life.

It was another bright, crisp day. He called Lincoln Peters at the bank where he worked and asked if he could count on taking Honoria when he left for Prague. Lincoln agreed that there was no reason for delay. One thing — the legal guardianship. Marion wanted to retain that a while longer. She was upset by the whole matter, and it would oil things if she felt that the situation was still in her control for another year. Charlie agreed, wanting only the tangible, visible child.

Then the question of a governess. Charles sat in a gloomy agency and talked to a cross Béarnaise and to a buxom Breton peasant, neither of whom he could have endured. There were others whom he would see tomorrow.

He lunched with Lincoln Peters at Griffons, trying to keep down his exultation.

"There's nothing quite like your own child," Lincoln said. "But you understand how Marion feels too."

"She's forgotten how hard I worked for seven years there," Charlie said. "She just remembers one night."

"There's another thing." Lincoln hesitated. "While you and Helen were tearing around Europe throwing money away, we were just getting along. I didn't touch any of the prosperity because I never got ahead enough to carry anything but my insurance. I think Marion felt there was some kind of injustice in it — you not even working toward the end, and getting richer and richer."

"It went just as quick as it came," said Charlie.

"Yes, a lot of it stayed in the hands of *chasseurs* and saxophone player and maîtres d'hôtel — well, the big party's over now. I just said that to explain Marion's feeling about those crazy years. If you drop in about six o'clock tonight before Marion's too tired, we'll settle the details on the spot."

Back at his hotel, Charlie found a *pneumatique* that had been redirected from the Ritz bar where Charlie had left his address for the purpose of finding a certain man.

> "DEAR CHARLIE: You were so strange when we saw you the other day that I wondered if I did something to offend you. If so, I'm not conscious of it. In fact, I have thought about you too much for the last year, and it's always been in the back of my mind that I might see you if I came over here. We *did* have such good times that crazy spring, like the night you and I stole the butcher's tricycle, and the time we tried to call on the president and you had the old derby rim and the wire cane. Everybody seems so old lately, but I don't feel old a bit. Couldn't we get together some time today for old time's sake? I've got a vile hang-over for the moment, but will be feeling better this afternoon and will look for you about five in the sweatshop at the Ritz.
>
> Always devotedly,
> LORRAINE."

His first feeling was one of awe that he had actually, in his mature years, stolen a tricycle and pedaled Lorraine all over the Étoile between the small hours and dawn. In retrospect it was a nightmare. Locking out Helen didn't fit in with any other act of his life, but the tricycle incident did — it was one of many. How many weeks or months of dissipation to arrive at that condition of utter irresponsibility?

He tried to picture how Lorraine had appeared to him then — very attractive; Helen was unhappy about it, though she

---

★ **on the spot** momentarily, right away
pneumatique (Fr., old) Rohrpost

derby rim (old) Rennfelge

sweatshop here: bar

small hours early hours of the morning
dissipation (old) the habit of wasting time and money

said nothing. Yesterday, in the restaurant, Lorraine had seemed trite, blurred, worn away. He emphatically did not want to see her, and he was glad Alix had not given away his hotel address. It was a relief to think, instead, of Honoria, to think of Sundays spent with her and of saying good morning to her and of knowing she was there in his house at night, drawing her breath in the darkness.

At five he took a taxi and bought presents for all the Peters — a piquant cloth doll, a box of Roman soldiers, flowers for Marion, big linen handkerchiefs for Lincoln.

He saw, when he arrived in the apartment, that Marion had accepted the inevitable. She greeted him now as though he were a recalcitrant member of the family, rather than a menacing outsider. Honoria had been told she was going; Charlie was glad to see that her tact made her conceal her excessive happiness. Only on his lap did she whisper her delight and the question "When?" before she slipped away with the other children.

He and Marion were alone for a minute in the room, and on an impulse he spoke out boldly:

"Family quarrels are bitter things. They don't go according to any rules. They're not like aches or wounds; they're more like splits in the skin that won't heal because there's not enough material. I wish you and I could be on better terms."

"Some things are hard to forget," she answered. "It's a question of confidence." There was no answer to this and presently she asked, "When do you propose to take her?"

"As soon as I can get a governess. I hoped the day after tomorrow."

"That's impossible. I've got to get her things in shape. Not before Saturday."

He yielded. Coming back into the room, Lincoln offered him a drink.

"I'll take my daily whisky," he said.

It was warm here, it was a home, people together by a fire. The children felt very safe and important; the mother and father were serious, watchful. They had things to do for the children more important than his visit here. A spoonful of medicine was, after all, more important than the strained relations between Marion and himself. They were not dull people, but they were very much in the grip of life and circumstances. He wondered if he couldn't do something to get Lincoln out of his rut at the bank.

A long peal at the door-bell; the *bonne à tout faire* passed through and went down the corridor. The door opened upon

---

trite very ordinary

recalcitrant stubborn and defiant

★ **to yield** to surrender; to agree to sth

rut here: boring routine job
peal ringing
bonne à tout faire (Fr.) Maid of all work

another long ring, and then voices, and the three in the salon looked up expectantly; Richard moved to bring the corridor within his range of vision, and Marion rose. Then the maid came back along the corridor, closely followed by the voices, which developed under the light into Duncan Schaeffer and Lorraine Quarrles.

They were gay, they were hilarious, they were roaring with laughter. For a moment Charlie was astounded; unable to understand how they ferreted out the Peters' address.

"Ah-h-h!" Duncan wagged his finger roguishly at Charlie. "Ah-h-h!"

They both slid down another cascade of laughter. Anxious and at a loss, Charlie shook hands with them quickly and presented them to Lincoln and Marion. Marion nodded, scarcely speaking. She had drawn back a step toward the fire; her little girl stood beside her, and Marion put an arm about her shoulder.

With growing annoyance at the intrusion, Charlie waited for them to explain themselves. After some concentration Duncan said:

intrusion interruption, invasion

"We came to invite you out to dinner. Lorraine and I insist that all this shishi, cagy business 'bout your address got to stop."

Charlie came closer to them, as if to force them backward down the corridor.

"Sorry, but I can't. Tell me where you'll be and I'll phone you in half an hour."

This made no impression. Lorraine sat down suddenly on the side of a chair, and focusing her eyes on Richard, cried, "Oh, what a nice little boy! Come here, little boy." Richard glanced at his mother, but did not move. With a perceptible shrug of her shoulders, Lorraine turned back to Charlie:

"Come and dine. Sure your cousins won' mine. See you so sel'om. Or solemn."

"I can't," said Charlie sharply. "You two have dinner and I'll phone you."

Her voice became suddenly unpleasant. "All right, we'll go. But I remember once when you hammered on my door at four A.M. I was enough of a good sport to give you a drink. Come on, Dunc."

Still in slow motion, with blurred, angry faces, with uncertain feet, they retired along the corridor.

"Good night," Charlie said.

"Good night!" responded Lorraine emphatically.

When he went back into the salon Marion had not moved, only now her son was standing in the circle of her other arm,

outrage Unverschämtheit

Lincoln was still swinging Honoria back and forth like a pendulum from side to side.

"What an outrage!" Charlie broke out. "What an absolute outrage!"

Neither of them answered, Charlie dropped into an armchair, picked up his drink, set it down again and said:

"People I haven't seen for two years having the colossal nerve —"

He broke off, Marion had made the sound "Oh!" in one swift, furious breath, turned her body from him with a jerk and left the room.

Lincoln set down Honoria carefully.

"You children go in and start your soup," he said, and when they obeyed, he said to Charlie:

"Marion's not well and she can't stand shocks. That kind of people make her really physically sick."

"I didn't tell them to come here. They wormed your name out of somebody. They deliberately —"

"Well, it's too bad. It doesn't help matters. Excuse me a minute."

Left alone, Charlie sat tense in his chair. In the next room he could hear the children eating, talking in monosyllables, already oblivious to the scene between their elders. He heard a murmur of conversation from a farther room and then the ticking bell of a telephone receiver picked up, and in a panic he moved to the other side of the room and out of earshot.

to be oblivious to sth to not notice sth

In a minute Lincoln came back. "Look here, Charlie. I think we'd better call off dinner for tonight. Marion's in bad shape."

"Is she angry with me?"

"Sort of," he said, almost roughly. "She's not strong and —"

"You mean she's changed her mind about Honoria?"

"She's pretty bitter right now. I don't know. You phone me at the bank tomorrow."

"I wish you'd explain to her I never dreamed these people would come here. I'm just as sore as you are."

"I couldn't explain anything to her now."

Charlie got up. He took his coat and hat and started down the corridor. Then he opened the door of the dining room and said in a strange voice, "Good night, children."

Honoria rose and ran around the table to hug him.

"Good night, sweetheart," he said vaguely, and then trying to make his voice more tender, trying to conciliate something, "Good night, dear children."

V

Charlie went directly to the Ritz bar with the furious idea of finding Lorraine and Duncan, but they were not there, and he realized that in any case there was nothing he could do. He had not touched his drink at the Peters, and now he ordered a whisky-and-soda. Paul came over to say hello.

"It's a great change," he said sadly. "We do about half the business we did. So many fellows I hear about back in the States lost everything, maybe not in the first crash, but then in the second. Your friend George Hardt lost every cent, I hear. Are you back in the States?"

"No, I'm in business in Prague."

"I heard that you lost a lot in the crash."

"I did," and he added grimly, "but I lost everything I wanted in the boom."

"Selling short."

"Something like that."

Again the memory of those days swept over him like a nightmare — the people they had met travelling; then people who couldn't add a row of figures or speak a coherent sentence. The little man Helen had consented to dance with at the ship's party, who had insulted her ten feet from the table; the women and girls carried screaming with drink or drugs out of public places —

— The men who locked their wives out in the snow, because the snow of twenty-nine wasn't real snow. If you didn't want it to be snow, you just paid some money.

He went to the phone and called the Peters' apartment; Lincoln answered.

"I called up because this thing is on my mind. Has Marion said anything definite?"

"Marion's sick," Lincoln answered shortly. "I know this thing isn't altogether your fault, but I can't have her go to pieces about it. I'm afraid we'll have to let it slide for six months; I can't take the chance of working her up to this state again."

"I see."

"I'm sorry, Charlie."

He went back to his table. His whisky glass was empty, but he shook his head when Alix looked at it questioningly. There wasn't much he could do now except send Honoria some things; he would send her a lot of things tomorrow. He thought rather angrily that this was just money — he had given so many people money. ...

"No, no more," he said to another waiter. "What do I owe you?"

Wall Street Crash of 1929
In 1929 the New York Stock Exchange saw an unprecedented crash that severely harmed the global economy and marked the beginning of the United States' decade-long Great Depression. On October 24 and 25, a.k.a. Black Monday and Black Tuesday, respectively, the stock market lost over $30 billion of its value.

to sell short (in banking) to sell securities that you expect to own at a later date and at a better price

He would come back some day; they couldn't make him pay forever. But he wanted his child, and nothing was much good now, beside that fact. He wasn't young any more, with a lot of nice thoughts and dreams to have by himself. He was absolutely sure Helen wouldn't have wanted him to be so alone.

The Norton Anthology of American Literature Vol. 2: 1865 to the Present. Eds. Nina Baym et al. Shorter 8th ed. New York: Norton, 2013, pp. 980–994.

One Friday Morning
Langston Hughes

The thrilling news did not come directly to Nancy Lee, but it came in little indirections that finally added themselves up to one tremendous fact: she had won the prize! But being a calm and quiet young lady, she did not say anything, although the whole high school buzzed with rumors, guesses, reportedly authentic announcements on the part of students who had no right to be making announcements at all — since no student really knew yet who had won this year's art scholarship.

But Nancy Lee's drawing was so good, her lines so sure, her colors so bright and harmonious, that certainly no other student in the senior art class at George Washington High was thought to have very much of a chance. Yet you never could tell. Last year nobody had expected Joe Williams to win the Artist Club scholarship with that funny modernistic water color he had done of the high-level bridge. In fact, it was hard to make out there was a bridge until you had looked at the picture a long time. Still, Joe Williams got the prize, was feted by the community's leading painters, club women, and society folks at a big banquet at the Park-Rose Hotel, and was now an award student at the Art School — the city's only art school. Nancy Lee Johnson was a colored girl, a few years out of the South. But seldom did her high-school classmates think of her as colored. She was smart, pretty and brown, and fitted in well with the life of the school. She stood high in scholarship, played a swell game of basketball, had taken part in the senior musical in a soft, velvety voice, and had never seemed to intrude or stand out, except in pleasant ways, so it was seldom even mentioned — her color.

Nancy Lee sometimes forgot she was colored herself. She liked her classmates and her school. Particularly she liked her art teacher, Miss Dietrich, the tall red-haired woman who taught her law and order in doing things; and the beauty of working step by step until a job is done; a picture finished; a design created; or a block print carved out of nothing but an idea and a smooth square of linoleum, inked, proofs made, and finally put down on paper — clean, sharp, beautiful, individual, unlike any other in the world, thus making the paper have a meaning nobody else could give it except Nancy Lee. That was the wonderful thing about true creation. You made something nobody else on earth could make — but you.

Miss Dietrich was the kind of teacher who brought out the

best in her students — but their own best, not anybody else's copied best. For anybody else's best, great though it might be, even Michelangelo's, wasn't enough to please Miss Dietrich, dealing with the creative impulses of young men and women living in an American city in the Middle West, and being American.

Nancy Lee was proud of being American, a Negro American with blood out of Africa a long time ago, too many generations back to count. But her parents had taught her the beauties of Africa, its strength, its song, its mighty rivers, its early smelting of iron, its building of the pyramids, and its ancient and important civilizations. And Miss Dietrich had discovered for her the sharp and humorous lines of African sculpture, Benin, Congo, Makonde. Nancy Lee's father was a mail carrier, her mother a social worker in a city settlement house. Both parents had been to Negro colleges in the South. And her mother had gotten a further degree in social work from a Northern university. Her parents were, like most Americans, simple, ordinary people who had worked hard and steadily for their education. Now they were trying to make it easier for Nancy Lee to achieve learning than it had been for them. They would be very happy when they heard of the award to their daughter — yet Nancy did not tell them. To surprise them would be better. Besides, there had been a promise.

Casually, one day, Miss Dietrich asked Nancy Lee what color frame she thought would be best on her picture. That had been the first inkling.

"Blue," Nancy Lee said. Although the picture had been entered in the Artist Club contest a month ago, Nancy Lee did not hesitate in her choice of color for the possible frame since she could still see her picture clearly in her mind's eye — for that picture waiting for the blue frame had come out of her soul, her own life, and had bloomed into miraculous being with Miss Dietrich's help. It was, she knew, the best water color she had painted in her four years as a high-school art student, and she was glad she had made something Miss Dietrich liked well enough to permit her to enter in the contest before she graduated.

It was not a modernistic picture in the sense that you had to look at it a long time to understand what it meant. It was just a simple scene in the city park on a spring day with the trees still leaflessly lacy against the sky, the new grass fresh and green, a flag on a tall pole in the center, children playing, and an old Negro woman sitting on a bench with her head turned. A lot for one picture, to be sure, but it was not there in heavy

---

Michelangelo (1475–1564), Florentine sculptor, painter and architect of the Renaissance period. Michelangelo is considered one of the greatest artists of all times.

Who are the introduced characters? What is the setting?

inkling hint, clue

to bloom here: to develop successfully

contest competition

lacy here: filigran

and final detail like a calendar. Its charm was that everything was light and airy, happy like spring, with a lot of blue sky, paper-white clouds, and air showing through. You could tell that the old Negro woman was looking at the flag, and that the flag was proud in the spring breeze, and that the breeze helped to make the children's dresses billow as they played. Miss Dietrich had taught Nancy Lee how to paint spring, people, and a breeze on what was only a plain white piece of paper from the supply closet. But Miss Dietrich had not said make it like any other spring-people-breeze ever seen before. She let it remain Nancy Lee's own. That is how the old Negro woman happened to be there looking at the flag — for in her mind the flag, the spring, and the woman formed a kind of triangle holding a dream Nancy Lee wanted to express. White stars on a blue field, spring, children, ever-growing life, and an old woman. Would the judges at the Artist Club like it?

One wet, rainy April afternoon Miss O'Shay, the girls' vice-principal, sent for Nancy Lee to stop by her office as school closed. Pupils without umbrellas or raincoats were clustered in doorways hoping to make it home between showers. Outside the skies were gray. Nancy Lee's thoughts were suddenly gray, too.

She did not think she had done anything wrong, yet that tight little knot came in her throat just the same as she approached Miss O'Shay's door. Perhaps she had banged her locker too often and too hard. Perhaps the note in French she had written to Sallie halfway across the study hall just for fun had never gotten to Sallie but into Miss O'Shay's hands instead. Or maybe she was failing in some subject and wouldn't be allowed to graduate. Chemistry! A pang went through the pit of her stomach.

She knocked on Miss O'Shay's door. That familiarly solid and competent voice said, "Come in."

Miss O'Shay had a way of making you feel welcome, even if you came to be expelled.

"Sit down, Nancy Lee Johnson," said Miss O'Shay. "I have something to tell you." Nancy Lee sat down. "But I must ask you to promise not to tell anyone yet."

"I won't, Miss O'Shay," Nancy Lee said, wondering what on earth the vice-principal had to say to her.

"You are about to graduate," Miss O'Shay said. "And we shall miss you. You have been an excellent student, Nancy, and you will not be without honors on the senior list, as I am sure you know."

At that point there was a light knock on the door.

to billow *sich bauschen*

supply closet a small room used for storing sth

vice-principal here: *stellvertretende Rektorin*

* **locker** *Schließfach*

to expel sb here: to force a student to leave school permanently

Miss O'Shay called out, "Come in," and Miss Dietrich entered. "May I be part of this, too?" she asked, tall and smiling.

"Of course," Miss O'Shay said. "I was just telling Nancy Lee what we thought of her. But I hadn't gotten around to giving her the news. Perhaps, Miss Dietrich, you'd like to tell her yourself."

Miss Dietrich was always direct. "Nancy Lee," she said, "your picture has won the Artist Club scholarship."

The slender brown girl's eyes widened, her heart jumped, then her throat tightened again. She tried to smile, but instead tears came to her eyes.

"Dear Nancy Lee," Miss O'Shay said, "we are so happy for you." The elderly white woman took her hand and shook it warmly while Miss Dietrich beamed with pride.

Nancy Lee must have danced all the way home. She never remembered quite how she got there through the rain. She hoped she had been dignified. But certainly she hadn't stopped to tell anybody her secret on the way. Raindrops, smiles, and tears mingled on her brown cheeks. She hoped her mother hadn't yet gotten home and that the house was empty. She wanted to have time to calm down and look natural before she had to see anyone. She didn't want to be bursting with excitement — having a secret to contain.

Miss O'Shay's calling her to the office had been in the nature of a preparation and a warning. The kind, elderly vice-principal said she did not believe in catching young ladies unawares, even with honors, so she wished her to know about the coming award. In making acceptance speeches she wanted her to be calm, prepared, not nervous, overcome, and frightened. So Nancy Lee was asked to think what she would say when the scholarship was conferred upon her a few days hence, both at the Friday morning high-school assembly hour, when the announcement would be made, and at the evening banquet of the Artist Club. Nancy Lee promised the vice-principal to think calmly about what she would say.

Miss Dietrich had then asked for some facts about her parents, her background, and her life, since such material would probably be desired for the papers. Nancy Lee had told her how, six years before, they had come up from the Deep South, her father having been successful in achieving a transfer from one post office to another, a thing he had long sought in order to give Nancy Lee a chance to go to school in the North. Now they lived in a modest Negro neighborhood, went to see the best plays when they came to town, and had been saving to send Nancy Lee to art school, in case she were permitted to enter. But the scholarship would help a great deal, for they were not rich people.

"Now Mother can have a new coat next winter," Nancy Lee thought, "because my tuition will be covered for the first year. And once in art school, there are other scholarships I can win." Dreams began to dance through her head, plans and ambitions, beauties she would create for herself, her parents, and the Negro people — for Nancy Lee possessed a deep and reverent race pride. She could see the old woman in her picture (really her grandmother in the South) lifting her head to the bright stars on the flag in the distance. A Negro in America! Often hurt, discriminated against, sometimes lynched — but always there were the stars on the blue body of the flag. Was there any other flag in the world that had so many stars? Nancy Lee thought deeply but she could remember none in all the encyclopedias or geographies she had ever looked into.

"Hitch your wagon to a star," Nancy Lee thought, dancing home in the rain. "Who were our flag makers?"

Friday morning came, the morning when the world would know — her high-school world, the newspaper world, her mother and dad. Dad could not be there at the assembly to hear the announcement, nor see her prize picture displayed on the stage, nor listen to Nancy Lee's little speech of acceptance, but Mother would be able to come, although Mother was much puzzled as to why Nancy Lee was so insistent she be at school on that particular Friday morning.

When something is happening, something new and fine, something that will change your very life, it is hard to go to sleep at night for thinking about it, and hard to keep your heart from pounding, or a strange little knot of joy from gathering in your throat. Nancy Lee had taken her bath, brushed her hair until it glowed, and had gone to bed thinking about the next day, the big day when, before three thousand students, she would be the one student honored, her painting the one painting to be acclaimed as the best of the year from all the art classes of the city. Her short speech of gratitude was ready. She went over it in her mind, not word for word (because she didn't want it to sound as if she had learned it by heart), but she let the thoughts flow simply and sincerely through her consciousness many times.

When the president of the Artist Club presented her with the medal and scroll of the scholarship award, she would say: "Judges and members of the Artist Club. I want to thank you for this award that means so much to me personally and through me to my people, the colored people of this city who,

★ **tuition** fees to be paid when studying

reverent full of respect or worship

Flag of the United States
A major symbol of US identity, the flag consists of two graphic segments: a blue rectangle in the upper left quarter containing fifty small white stars, and thirteen horizontal stripes of red alternating with white. In its current design, marking Hawaii's admission in 1959, the stars represent the fifty American states, while the stripes stand for the thirteen British colonies that declared independence. The flag's nicknames include "The Stars and Stripes" and "The Star-Spangled Banner".

to hitch one's wagon to a star to set high goals (from a phrase by Ralph Waldo Emerson in his 1862 essay "American Civilization")

assembly (fml.) meeting, gathering

Pledge of Allegiance
In the Pledge of Allegiance, Americans ritually express their connection and loyalty to the United States. It is common practice to recite the Pledge at the beginning of the school day and in congressional meetings. The current version reads: "I pledge allegiance to the Flag of the United States, and to the Republic for which it stands, one Nation under God, indivisible, with liberty and justice for all."

★ **creed** religious belief

sometimes, are discouraged and bewildered, thinking that color and poverty are against them. I accept this award with gratitude and pride, not for myself alone, but for my race that believes in American opportunity and American fairness — and the bright stars in our flag. I thank Miss Dietrich and the teachers who made it possible for me to have the knowledge and training that lie behind this honor you have conferred upon my painting. When I came here from the South a few years ago, I was not sure how you would receive me. You received me well. You have given me a chance and helped me along the road I wanted to follow. I suppose the judges know that every week here at assembly the students of this school pledge allegiance to the flag. I shall try to be worthy of that pledge, and of the help and friendship and understanding of my fellow citizens of whatever race or creed, and of our American dream of 'Liberty and justice for all!'"

That would be her response before the students in the morning. How proud and happy the Negro pupils would be, perhaps almost as proud as they were of the one colored star on the football team. Her mother would probably cry with happiness. Thus Nancy Lee went to sleep dreaming of a wonderful tomorrow.

The bright sunlight of an April morning woke her. There was breakfast with her parents — their half-amused and puzzled faces across the table, wondering what could be this secret that made her eyes so bright. The swift walk to school; the clock in the tower almost nine; hundreds of pupils streaming into the long, rambling old building that was the city's largest high school; the sudden quiet of the homeroom after the bell rang; then the teacher opening her record book to call the roll. But just before she began, she looked across the room until her eyes located Nancy Lee.

"Nancy," she said, "Miss O'Shay would like to see you in her office, please."

Nancy Lee rose and went out while the names were being called and the word *present* added its period to each name. Perhaps, Nancy Lee thought, the reporters from the papers had already come. Maybe they wanted to take her picture before assembly, which wasn't until ten o'clock. (Last year they had had the photograph of the winner of the award in the morning papers as soon as the announcement had been made.) Nancy Lee knocked at Miss O'Shay's door.

"Come in."

The vice-principal stood at her desk. There was no one else in the room. It was very quiet.

"Sit down, Nancy Lee," she said. Miss O'Shay did not smile. There was a long pause. The seconds went by slowly. "I do not know how to tell you what I have to say," the elderly woman began, her eyes on the papers on her desk. "I am indignant and ashamed for myself and for this city." Then she lifted her eyes and looked at Nancy Lee in the neat blue dress sitting there before her. "You are not to receive the scholarship this morning."

Outside in the hall the electric bells announcing the first period rang, loud and interminably long. Miss O'Shay remained silent. To the brown girl there in the chair, the room grew suddenly smaller, smaller, smaller, and there was no air. She could not speak.

Miss O'Shay said, "When the committee learned that you were colored, they changed their plans."

Still Nancy Lee said nothing, for there was no air to give breath to her lungs.

"Here is the letter from the committee, Nancy Lee." Miss O'Shay picked it up and read the final paragraph to her.

"'It seems to us wiser to arbitrarily rotate the award among the various high schools of the city from now on. And especially in this case since the student chosen happens to be colored, a circumstance which unfortunately, had we known, might have prevented this embarrassment. But there have never been any Negro students in the local art school, and the presence of one there might create difficulties for all concerned. We have high regard for the quality of Nancy Lee Johnson's talent, but we do not feel it would be fair to honor it with the Artist Club award.'" Miss O'Shay paused. She put the letter down.

"Nancy Lee, I am very sorry to have to give you this message."

"But my speech," Nancy Lee said, "was about ..." The words stuck in her throat. "... about America."

Miss O'Shay had risen, she turned her back and stood looking out the window at the spring tulips in the school yard.

"I thought, since the award would be made at assembly right after our oath of allegiance," the words tumbled almost hysterically from Nancy Lee's throat now, "I would put part of the flag salute in my speech. You know, Miss O'Shay, that part of 'liberty and justice for all.'"

"I know," said Miss O'Shay slowly facing the room again. "But America is only what we who believe in it, make it. I am Irish. You may not know, Nancy Lee, but years ago we were called the dirty Irish, and mobs rioted against us in the big cities, and we were invited to go back where we came from. But we didn't

indignant angry

arbitrarily randomly, by chance

★ **embarrassment** sth that causes a feeling of being uncomfortable or ashamed

oath Schwur

go. And we didn't give up, because we believed in the American dream, and in our power to make that dream come true. Difficulties, yes. Mountains to climb, yes. Discouragements to face, yes. Democracy to make, yes. That is it, Nancy Lee! We still have in this world of ours democracy to *make*. You and I, Nancy Lee. But the premise and the base are here, the lines of the Declaration of Independence and the words of Lincoln are here, and the stars in our flag. Those who deny you this scholarship do not know the meaning of those stars, but it's up to us to make them know. As a teacher in the public schools of this city, I myself will go before the school board and ask them to remove from our system the offer of any prizes or awards denied to any student because of race or color."

Suddenly Miss O'Shay stopped speaking. Her clear, clear blue eyes looked into those of the girl before her. The woman's eyes were full of strength and courage. "Lift up your head, Nancy Lee, and smile at me."

Miss O'Shay stood against the open window with the green lawn and the tulips beyond, the sunlight tangled in her gray hair, her voice an electric flow of strength to the hurt spirit of Nancy Lee. The Abolitionists who believed in freedom when there was slavery must have been like that. The first white teachers who went into the Deep South to teach the freed slaves must have been like that. All those who stand against ignorance, narrowness, hate, and mud on stars must be like that.

Nancy Lee lifted her head and smiled. The bell for assembly rang. She went through the long hall filled with students toward the auditorium.

"There will be other awards," Nancy Lee thought. "There're schools in other cities. This won't keep me down. But when I'm a woman, I'll fight to see that these things don't happen to other girls as this has happened to me. And men and women like Miss O'Shay will help me."

She took her seat among the seniors. The doors of the auditorium closed. As the principal came onto the platform, the students rose and turned their eyes to the flag on the stage.

One hand went to the heart, the other outstretched toward the flag. Three thousand voices spoke. Among them was the voice of a dark girl whose cheeks were suddenly wet with tears, "… one nation indivisible, with liberty and justice for all."

"That is the land we must make," she thought.

The Short Stories of Langston Hughes. Ed. Akiba Sullivan Harper, 1st paperback ed. New York: Hill & Wang, a division of Farrar, Straus and Giroux, 1997, pp. 153–162.

Tony's Story
Leslie Marmon Silko

ONE

It happened one summer when the sky was wide and hot and the summer rains did not come; the sheep were thin, and the tumbleweeds turned brown and died. Leon came back from the army. I saw him standing by the Ferris wheel across from the people who came to sell melons and chili on San Lorenzo's Day. He yelled at me, "Hey Tony — over here!" I was embarrassed to hear him yell so loud, but then I saw the wine bottle with the brown-paper sack crushed around it.

"How's it going, buddy?"

He grabbed my hand and held it tight like a white man. He was smiling. "It's good to be home again. They asked me to dance tomorrow — it's only the Corn Dance, but I hope I haven't forgotten what to do."

"You'll remember — it will all come back to you when you hear the drum." I was happy, because I knew that Leon was once more a part of the pueblo. The sun was dusty and low in the west, and the procession passed by us, carrying San Lorenzo back to his niche in the church.

"Do you want to get something to eat?" I asked.

Leon laughed and patted the bottle. "No, you're the only one who needs to eat. Take this dollar — they're selling hamburgers over there." He pointed past the merry-go-round to a stand with cotton candy and a snow-cone machine.

It was then that I saw the cop pushing his way through the crowds of people gathered around the hamburger stand and bingo-game tent; he came steadily toward us. I remembered Leon's wine and looked to see if the cop was watching us; but he was wearing dark glasses and I couldn't see his eyes.

He never said anything before he hit Leon in the face with his fist. Leon collapsed into the dust, and the paper sack floated in the wine and pieces of glass. He didn't move and blood kept bubbling out of his mouth and nose. I could hear a siren. People crowded around Leon and kept pushing me away. The tribal policemen knelt over Leon and one of them looked up at the state cop and asked what was going on. The big cop didn't answer. He was staring at the little patterns of blood in the dust near Leon's mouth. The dust soaked up the blood almost before it dripped to the ground — it had been a very dry summer. The cop didn't leave until they laid Leon in the back of the paddy wagon.

---

tumbleweed round plant that grows in dry areas; *Steppenläufer*

Ferris wheel big vertical wheel at an amusement park, *Riesenrad*

San Lorenzo's Day August 10th; the martyr Saint Lawrence is of particular importance to Spanish Catholicism

pueblo (Sp.) village; here: community of Native Americans in the Southwest US

⬆ How does Tony perceive Leon?

to pat to touch sth to draw attention to it

merry-go-round *Karussell*

snow cone dessert of flavoured crushed ice, served in paper cones or foam cups

paddy wagon large police van used for carrying prisoners

The moon was already high when we got to the hospital in Albuquerque. We waited a long time outside the emergency room with Leon propped between us. Siow and Gaisthea kept asking me, "What happened, what did Leon say to the cop?" and I told them how we were just standing there, ready to buy hamburgers — we'd never even seen him before. They put stitches around Leon's mouth and gave him a shot; he was lucky, they said — it could've been a broken jaw instead of broken teeth.

TWO

They dropped me off near my house. The moon had moved lower into the west and left the close rows of houses in long shadows. Stillness breathed around me, and I wanted to run from the feeling behind me in the dark; the stories about witches ran with me. That night I had a dream — the big cop was pointing a long bone at me — they always use human bones, and the whiteness flashed silver in the moonlight where he stood. He didn't have a human face — only little, round, white-rimmed eyes on a black ceremonial mask.

Leon was better in a few days. But he was bitter, and all he could talk about was the cop. "I'll kill the big bastard if he comes around here again," Leon kept saying.

With something like the cop it is better to forget, and I tried to make Leon understand. "It's over now. There's nothing you can do."

I wondered why men who came back from the army were troublemakers on the reservation. Leon even took it before the pueblo meeting. They discussed it, and the old men decided that Leon shouldn't have been drinking. The interpreter read a passage out of the revised pueblo law-and-order code about possessing intoxicants on the reservation, so we got up and left.

Then Leon asked me to go with him to Grants to buy a roll of barbed wire for his uncle. On the way we stopped at Cerritos for gas, and I went into the store for some pop. He was inside. I stopped in the doorway and turned around before he saw me, but if he really was what I feared, then he would not need to see me — he already knew we were there. Leon was waiting with the truck engine running almost like he knew what I would say. "Let's go — the big cop's inside."

Leon gunned it and the pickup skidded back on the highway. He glanced back in the rear-view mirror. "I didn't see his car."

"Hidden," I said.

Leon shook his head. "He can't do it again. We are just as good as them." The guys who came back always talked like that.

THREE

The sky was hot and empty. The half-grown tumbleweeds were dried-up flat and brown beside the highway, and across the valley heat shimmered above wilted fields of corn. Even the mountains high beyond the pale sandrock mesas were dusty blue. I was afraid to fall asleep so I kept my eyes on the blue mountains — not letting them close — soaking in the heat; and then I knew why the drought had come that summer.

Leon shook me. "He's behind us — the cop's following us!"

I looked back and saw the red light on top of the car whirling around, and I could make out the dark image of a man, but where the face should have been there were only the silvery lenses of the dark glasses he wore.

"Stop, Leon! He wants us to stop!"

Leon pulled over and stopped on the narrow gravel shoulder. "What in the hell does he want?" Leon's hands were shaking. Suddenly the cop was standing beside the truck, gesturing for Leon to roll down his window. He pushed his head inside, grinding the gum in his mouth; the smell of Doublemint was all around us.

"Get out. Both of you."

I stood beside Leon in the dry weeds and tall yellow grass that broke through the asphalt and rattled in the wind. The cop studied Leon's driver's license. I avoided his face — I knew that I couldn't look at his eyes, so I stared at his black half-Wellingtons, with the black uniform cuffs pulled over them; but my eyes kept moving, upward past the black gun belt. My legs were quivering, and I tried to keep my eyes away from his. But it was like the time when I was very little and my parents warned me not to look into the masked dancers' eyes because they would grab me, and my eyes would not stop.

"What's your name?" His voice was high-pitched and it distracted me from the meaning of the words. I remember Leon said, "He doesn't understand English so good," and finally I said that I was Antonio Sousea, while my eyes strained to look beyond the silver frosted glasses that he wore; but only my distorted face and squinting eyes reflected back.

And then the cop stared at us for a while, silent; finally he laughed and chewed his gum some more slowly. "Where were you going?"

"To Grants." Leon spoke English very clearly. "Can we go now?"

wilted *welk*

mesa *(AE) small area of flat high land*

gravel shoulder *Schotterstreifen*

Wellington *Gummistiefel*

★ **to distract sb** *(from sth) jmdn. (von etw.) ablenken*
distracted *abgelenkt, zerstreut, verwirrt*
distracting *disturbing*
distraction *disturbance; Ablenkung*

to strain *to try hard by using strength*

Leon was twisting the key chain around his fingers, and I felt the sun everywhere. Heat swelled up from the asphalt and when cars went by, hot air and motor smell rushed past us.

"I don't like smart guys, Indian. It's because of you bastards that I'm here. They transferred me here because of Indians. They thought there wouldn't be as many for me here. But I find them." He spit his gum into the weeds near my foot and walked back to the patrol car. It kicked up gravel and dust when he left.

We got back in the pickup, and I could taste sweat in my mouth, so I told Leon that we might as well go home since he would be waiting for us up ahead.

"He can't do this." Leon said. "We've got a right to be on this highway."

I couldn't understand why Leon kept talking about "rights", because it wasn't "rights" that he was after, but Leon didn't seem to understand; he couldn't remember the stories that old Teofilo told.

I didn't feel safe until we turned off the highway and I could see the pueblo and my own house. It was noon, and everybody was eating — the village seemed empty — even the dogs had crawled away from the heat. The door was open, but there was only silence, and I was afraid that something had happened to all of them. Then as soon as I opened the screen door the little kids started crying for more Kool-Aid, and my mother said "no," and it was noisy again like always. Grandfather commented that it had been a fast trip to Grants, and I said "yeah" and didn't explain because it would've only worried them.

"Leon goes looking for trouble — I wish you wouldn't hang around with him." My father didn't like trouble. But I knew that the cop was something terrible, and even to speak about it risked bringing it close to all of us; so I didn't say anything. That afternoon Leon spoke with the Governor, and he promised to send letters to the Bureau of Indian Affairs and to the State Police Chief. Leon seemed satisfied with that. I reached into my pocket for the arrowhead on the piece of string.

"What's that for?"

I held it out to him. "Here, wear it around your neck — like mine. See? Just in case," I said, "for protection."

"You don't believe in *that*, do you?" He pointed to a .30-30 leaning against the wall. "I'll take this with me whenever I'm in the pickup."

"But you can't be sure that it will kill one of them."

Leon looked at me and laughed. "What's the matter," he said,

---

screen door door with a wire net to keep insects out
Kool-Aid popular brand of flavoured drink mix

arrowhead Pfeilspitze

"have they brainwashed you into believing that a .30-30 wouldn't kill a white man?" He handed back the arrowhead. Here, you wear two of them."

to brainwash sb to force sb to believe sth

⬆ Why does Leon reject the arrowhead?

FOUR

Leon's uncle asked me if I wanted to stay at the sheep camp for a while. The lambs were big, and there wouldn't be much for me to do, so I told him I would. We left early, while the sun was still low and red in the sky. The highway was empty, and I sat there beside Leon imagining what it was like before there were highways or even horses. Leon turned off the highway onto the sheep-camp road that climbs around the sandstone mesas until suddenly all the trees are piñons.

piñon (Sp.) *Kiefer*

Leon glanced in the rear-view mirror. "He's following us!"
My body began to shake and I wasn't sure if I would be able to speak. "There's no place left to hide. It follows us everywhere."
Leon looked at me like he didn't understand what I'd said. Then I looked past Leon and saw that the patrol car had pulled up beside us; the piñon branches were whipping and scraping the side of the truck as it tried to force us off the road. Leon kept driving with the two right wheels in the rut — bumping and scraping the trees. Leon never looked over at it so he couldn't have known how the reflections kept moving across the mirror-lenses of the dark glasses. We were in the narrow canyon with pale sandstone close on either side — the canyon that ended with a spring where willows and grass and tiny blue flowers grow.

to pull up here: to stop a car

willow *Weide*

"We've got to kill it, Leon. We must burn the body to be sure." Leon didn't seem to be listening. I kept wishing that old Teofilo could have been there to chant the proper words while we did it. Leon stopped the truck and got out — he still didn't understand what it was. I sat in the pickup with the .30-30 across my lap, and my hands were slippery.

to chant to sing using a limited range of notes

The big cop was standing in front of the pickup, facing Leon. "You made your mistake, Indian. I'm going to beat the shit out of you." He raised the billy club slowly. "I like to beat Indians with this."

billy club *Schlagstock*

He moved toward Leon with the stick raised high, and it was like the long bone in my dream when he pointed it at me — a human bone painted brown to look like wood, to hide what it really was; they'll do that, you know — carve the bone into a spoon and use it around the house until the victim comes within range.

The shot sounded far away and I couldn't remember aiming.

wand stick used for doing magic

glossy shiny

to wobble to rock slightly from side to side

But he was motionless on the ground and the bone wand lay near his feet. The tumbleweeds and tall yellow grass were sprayed with glossy, bright blood. He was on his back, and the sand between his legs and long his left side was soaking up the dark, heavy blood — it had not rained for a long time, and even the tumbleweeds were dying.

"Tony! You killed him — you killed the cop."

"Help me! We'll set the car on fire."

Leon acted strange, and he kept looking at me like he wanted to run. The head wobbled and swung back and forth, and the left hand and the legs left individual trails in the sand. The face was the same. The dark glasses hadn't fallen off and they blinded me with their hot-sun reflections until I pushed the body into the front seat.

The gas tank exploded and the flames spread along the underbelly of the car. The tires filled the wide sky with spirals of thick black smoke.

"My God, Tony. What's wrong with you? That's a state cop you killed." Leon was pale and shaking.

I wiped my hands on my Levis. "Don't worry, everything is O.K. now, Leon. It's killed. They sometimes take on strange forms."

The tumbleweeds around the car caught fire, and little heat-waves shimmered up toward the sky; in the west, rain clouds were gathering.

_{The Scribner Anthology of Contemporary Short Fiction: 50 North America Short Stories since 1970. Eds. Lex Williford, Michael Martone. 2nd ed. New York: Touchstone, 2007, pp. 579–584.}

Sexy
Jhumpa Lahiri

It was a wife's worst nightmare. After nine years of marriage, Laxmi told Miranda, her cousin's husband had fallen in love with another woman. He sat next to her on a plane, on a flight from Delhi to Montreal, and instead of flying home to his wife and son, he got off with the woman at Heathrow. He called his wife, and told her he'd had a conversation that had changed his life, and that he needed time to figure things out. Laxmi's cousin had taken to her bed.

"Not that I blame her," Laxmi said. She reached for the Hot Mix she munched throughout the day, which looked to Miranda like dusty orange cereal. "Imagine. An English girl, half his age." Laxmi was only a few years older than Miranda, but she was already married, and kept a photo of herself and her husband, seated on a white stone bench in front of the Taj Mahal, tacked to the inside of her cubicle, which was next to Miranda's. Laxmi had been on the phone for at least an hour, trying to calm her cousin down. No one noticed; they worked for a public radio station, in the fund-raising department, and were surrounded by people who spent all day on the phone, soliciting pledges.

"I feel worst for the boy," Laxmi added. "He's been at home for days. My cousin said she can't even take him to school."

"It sounds awful," Miranda said. Normally Laxmi's phone conversations — mainly to her husband, about what to cook for dinner — distracted Miranda as she typed letters, asking members of the radio station to increase their annual pledge in exchange for a tote bag or an umbrella. She could hear Laxmi clearly, her sentences peppered every now and then with an Indian word, through the laminated wall between their desks. But that afternoon Miranda hadn't been listening. She'd been on the phone herself, with Dev, deciding where to meet later that evening.

"Then again, a few days at home won't hurt him." Laxmi ate some more Hot Mix, then put it away in a drawer. "He's something of a genius. He has a Punjabi mother and a Bengali father, and because he learns French and English at school he already speaks four languages. I think he skipped two grades." Dev was Bengali, too. At first, Miranda thought it was a religion. But then he pointed it out to her, a place in India called Bengal, on a map printed in an issue of *The Economist*. He had brought the magazine specially to her apartment, for she did

---

Taj Mahal
The Taj Mahal is a white marble mausoleum located in the Indian city of Agra. In 1632 the emperor Shah Jahan commissioned the monumental building to honour his wife Mumtaz Mahal. A UNESCO World Heritage Site since 1983, it has been considered a landmark of Muslim architecture and art in India.

cubicle small enclosed area in an office

to solicit pledges to ask sb for funds or donations

* to distract sb jmdn. ablenken

tote bag cloth bag

Punjabi from Punjab, a state in northern India
Bengali from Bengal, a region that covers parts of India and Bangladesh
* to skip a grade (a class) eine Klasse überspringen
The Economist weekly British news magazine

not own an atlas, or any other books with maps in them. He'd pointed to the city where he'd been born, and another city where his father had been born. One of the cities had a box around it, intended to attract the reader's eye. When Miranda asked what the box indicated, Dev rolled up the magazine and said, "Nothing you'll ever need to worry about," and he tapped her playfully on the head.

Before leaving her apartment, he'd tossed the magazine in the garbage, along with the ends of the three cigarettes he always smoked in the course of his visits. But after she watched his car disappear down Commonwealth Avenue, back to his house in the suburbs, where he lived with his wife, Miranda retrieved it, and brushed the ashes off the cover, and rolled it in the opposite direction to get it to lie flat. She got into bed, still rumpled from their lovemaking, and studied the borders of Bengal. There was a bay below and mountains above. The map was connected to an article about something called the Gramin Bank. She turned the page, hoping for a photograph of the city where Dev was born, but all she found were graphs and grids. Still, she stared at them, thinking the whole while about Dev, about how only fifteen minutes ago he'd propped her feet on top of his shoulders, and pressed her knees to her chest, and told her that he couldn't get enough of her.

She'd met him a week ago, at Filene's. She was there on her lunch break, buying discounted pantyhose in the Basement. Afterward she took the escalator to the main part of the store, to the cosmetics department, where soaps and creams were displayed like jewels, and eye shadows and powders shimmered like butterflies pinned behind protective glass. Though Miranda had never bought anything other than a lipstick, she liked walking through the cramped, confined maze, which was familiar to her in a way the rest of Boston still was not. She liked negotiating her way past the women planted at every turn, who sprayed cards with perfume and waved them in the air; sometimes she would find a card days afterward, folded in her coat pocket, and the rich aroma, still faintly preserved, would warm her as she waited on cold mornings for the T.

That day, stopping to smell one of the more pleasing cards, Miranda noticed a man standing at one of the counters. He held a slip of paper covered in a precise, feminine hand. A saleswoman took one look at the paper and began to open drawers. She produced an oblong cake of soap in a black case, a hydrating mask, a vial of cell renewal drops, and two tubes of face cream. The man was tanned, with black hair that was visible on his knuckles. He wore a flamingo pink shirt, a navy blue suit, a camel overcoat with gleaming leather buttons. In order to pay he had taken off pigskin gloves. Crisp bills emerged from a burgundy wallet. He didn't wear a wedding ring.

"What can I get you, honey?" the saleswoman asked Miranda. She looked over the tops of her tortoiseshell glasses, assessing Miranda's complexion.

Miranda didn't know what she wanted. All she knew was that she didn't want the man to walk away. He seemed to be lingering, waiting, along with the saleswoman, for her to say something. She stared at some bottles, some short, others tall, arranged on an oval tray, like a family posing for a photograph.

"A cream," Miranda said eventually.

"How old are you?"

"Twenty-two."

The saleswoman nodded, opening a frosted bottle. "This may seem a bit heavier than what you're used to, but I'd start now. All your wrinkles are going to form by twenty-five. After that they just start showing."

While the saleswoman dabbed the cream on Miranda's face, the man stood and watched. While Miranda was told the proper way to apply it, in swift upward strokes beginning at the base of her throat, he spun the lipstick carousel. He pressed a pump that dispensed cellulite gel and massaged it into the back of his ungloved hand. He opened a jar, leaned over, and drew so close that a drop of cream flecked his nose.

Miranda smiled, but her mouth was obscured by a large brush that the saleswoman was sweeping over her face. "This is blusher Number Two," the woman said. "Gives you some color."

Miranda nodded, glancing at her reflection in one of the angled mirrors that lined the counter. She had silver eyes and skin pale as paper, and the contrast with her hair, as dark and glossy as an espresso bean, caused people to describe her as striking, if not pretty. She had a narrow, egg-shaped head that rose to a prominent point. Her features, too, were narrow, with nostrils so slim that they appeared to have been pinched with a clothespin. Now her face glowed, rosy at the cheeks, smoky below the brow bone. Her lips glistened.

The man was glancing in a mirror, too, quickly wiping the cream from his nose. Miranda wondered where he was from. She thought he might be Spanish, or Lebanese. When he opened another jar, and said, to no one in particular, "This one smells like pineapple," she detected only the hint of an accent.

"Anything else for you today?" the saleswoman asked, accepting Miranda's credit card.

---

crisp bills *druckfrische Banknoten*

complexion appearance of the skin on your face

wrinkle *Falte*

jar glass container with a lid

blusher *Rouge*

*** to glance at sb/sth** *einen Blick auf jmdn./etw. werfen*

nostril *Nasenloch*
clothespin (AE) *Wäscheklammer*

"No thanks."
The woman wrapped the cream in several layers of red tissue. "You'll be very happy with this product." Miranda's hand was unsteady as she signed the receipt. The man hadn't budged. "I threw in a sample of our new eye gel," the saleswoman added, handling Miranda a small shopping bag. She looked at Miranda's credit card before sliding it across the counter. "Bye-bye, Miranda."
Miranda began walking. At first she sped up. Then, noticing the doors that led to Downtown Crossing, she slowed down. "Part of your name is Indian," the man said, pacing his steps with hers.
She stopped, as did he, at a circular table piled with sweaters, flanked with pinecones and velvet bows. "Miranda?"
"Mira. I have an aunt named Mira."
His name was Dev. He worked in an investment bank back that way he said, tilting his head in the direction of South Station. He was the first man with a mustache, Miranda decided, she found handsome.
They walked together toward Park Street station, past the kiosks that sold cheap belts and handbags. A fierce January wind spoiled the part in her hair. As she fished for a token in her coat pocket, her eyes fell to his shopping bag. "And those are for her?"
"Who?"
"Your Aunt Mira."
"They're for my wife." He uttered the words slowly, holding Miranda's gaze. "She's going to India for a few weeks." He rolled his eyes. "She's addicted to this stuff."

Somehow, without the wife there, it didn't seem so wrong. At first Miranda and Dev spent every night together, almost. He explained that he couldn't spend the whole night at her place, because his wife called every day at six in the morning, from India, where it was four in the afternoon. And so he left her apartment at two, three, often as late as four in the morning, driving back to his house in the suburbs. During the day he called her every hour, it seemed, from work, or from his cell phone. Once he learned Miranda's schedule he left her a message each evening at five-thirty, when she was on the T coming back to her apartment, just so, he said, she could hear his voice as soon as she walked through the door. "I'm thinking about you," he'd say on the tape. "I can't wait to see you." He told her he liked spending time in her apartment, with its kitchen counter no wider than a breadbox, and scratchy floors that sloped, and a buzzer in the lobby, that always made a slightly embarrassing sound when he pressed it. He said he admired her for moving to Boston, where she knew no one, instead of remaining in Michigan, where she'd grown up and gone to college. When Miranda told him it was nothing to admire, that she'd moved to Boston precisely for that reason, he shook his head. "I know what it's like to be lonely," he said, suddenly serious, and at that moment Miranda felt that he understood her — understood how she felt some nights on the T, after seeing a movie on her own, or going to a bookstore to read magazines, or having drinks with Laxmi, who always had to meet her husband at Alewife station in an hour or two. In less serious moments Dev said he liked that her legs were longer than her torso, something he'd observed the first time she walked across a room naked. "You're the first," he told her, admiring her from the bed. "The first woman I've known with legs this long."

Dev was the first to tell her that. Unlike the boys she dated in college, who were simply taller, heavier versions of the ones she dated in high school, Dev was the first always to pay for things, and hold doors open, and reach across a table in a restaurant to kiss her hand. He was the first to bring her a bouquet of flowers so immense she'd had to split it up into all six of her drinking glasses, and the first to whisper her name again and again when they made love. Within days of meeting him, when she was at work, Miranda began to wish that there were a picture of her and Dev tacked to the inside of her cubicle, like the one of Laxmi and her husband in front of the Taj Mahal. She didn't tell Laxmi about Dev. She didn't tell anyone. Part of her wanted to tell Laxmi, if only because Laxmi was Indian, too. But Laxmi was always on the phone with her cousin these days, who was still in bed, whose husband was still in London, and whose son still wasn't going to school. "You must eat something," Laxmi would urge. "You mustn't lose your health." When she wasn't speaking to her cousin, she spoke to her husband, shorter conversations, in which she ended up arguing about whether to have chicken or lamb for dinner. "I'm sorry," Miranda heard her apologize at one point. "This whole thing just makes me a little paranoid."

Miranda and Dev didn't argue. They went to movies at the Nickelodeon and kissed the whole time. They ate pulled pork and cornbread in Davis Square, a paper napkin tucked like a cravat into the collar of Dev's shirt. They sipped sangria at the bar of a Spanish restaurant, a grinning pig's head presiding over their conversation. They went to the MFA and picked out

to urge (sb to do sth) to strongly advise
urgent sth that needs to be dealt with immediately
urgently dringend
urgency Dringlichkeit

pulled pork popular American barbecue dish

MFA Museum of Fine Arts, Boston

a poster of water lilies for her bedroom. One Saturday, following an afternoon concert at Symphony Hall, he showed her his favorite place in the city, the Mapparium at the Christian Science center, where they stood inside a room made of glowing stained-glass panels, which was shaped like the inside of a globe, but looked like the outside of one. In the middle of the room was a transparent bridge, so that it felt as it they were standing in the center of the world. Dev pointed to India, which was red, and far more detailed than the map in *The Economist*. He explained that many of the countries, like Siam and Italian Somaliland, no longer existed in the same way; the names had changed by now. The ocean, as blue as a peacock's breast, appeared in two shades, depending on the depth of the water. He showed her the deepest spot on earth, seven miles deep, above the Mariana Islands. They peered over the bridge and saw the Antarctic archipelago at their feet, craned their necks and saw a giant metal star overhead. As Dev spoke, his voice bounced wildly off the glass, sometimes loud, sometimes soft, sometimes seeming to land in Miranda's chest, sometimes eluding her ear altogether. When a group of tourists walked onto the bridge, she could hear them clearing their throats, as if through microphones. Dev explained that it was because of the acoustics.

Miranda found London, where Laxmi's cousin's husband was, with the woman he'd met on the plane. She wondered which of the cities in India Dev's wife was in. The farthest Miranda had ever been was to the Bahamas once when she was a child. She searched but couldn't find it on the glass panels. When the tourists left and she and Dev were alone again, he told her to stand at one end of the bridge. Even though they were thirty feet apart, Dev said, they'd be able to hear each other whisper.

"I don't believe you," Miranda said. It was the first time she'd spoken since they'd entered. She felt as if speakers were embedded in her ears.

"Go ahead," he urged, walking backward to his end of the bridge. His voice dropped to a whisper. "Say something." She watched his lips forming the words; at the same time she heard them so clearly that she felt them under her skin, under her winter coat, so near and full of warmth that she felt herself go hot.

"Hi," she whispered, unsure of what else to say.

"You're sexy," he whispered back.

At work the following week, Laxmi told Miranda that it wasn't

---

Mapparium
The Mapparium is the chief attraction of Boston's Mary Baker Eddy Library. It is a three-story tall globe made of stained glass, allowing visitors to walk through the structure and view the geography of the earth. Built in 1935, the Mapparium displays the world's political order of that time.

Siam, Italian Somaliland presently Thailand and Somalia

Mariana Islands island chain in the western Pacific Ocean

* **to bounce** to jump, to rebound; here: to reverberate; *widerhallen*

Why does Miranda feel that her relationship with Dev is something completely new?

the first time her cousin's husband had had an affair. "She's decided to let him come to his senses," Laxmi said one evening as they were getting ready to leave the office. "She says it's for the boy. She's willing to forgive him for the boy." Miranda waited as Laxmi shut off her computer. "He'll come crawling back, and she'll let him," Laxmi said, shaking her head. "Not me. If my husband so much as looked at another woman I'd change the locks." She studied the picture tacked to her cubicle. Laxmi's husband had his arm draped over her shoulder, his knees leaning in toward her on the bench. She turned to Miranda. "Wouldn't you?"

She nodded. Dev's wife was coming back from India the next day. That afternoon he'd called Miranda at work, to say he had to go to the airport to pick her up. He promised he'd call as soon as he could.

"What's the Taj Mahal like?" she asked Laxmi.

"The most romantic spot on earth." Laxmi's face brightened at the memory. "An everlasting monument to love."

While Dev was at the airport, Miranda went to Filene's Basement to buy herself things she thought a mistress should have. She found a pair of black high heels with buckles smaller than a baby's teeth. She found a satin slip with scalloped edges and a knee-length silk robe. Instead of the pantyhose she normally wore to work, she found sheer stockings with a seam. She searched through piles and wandered through racks, pressing back hanger after hanger, until she found a cocktail dress made of a slinky silvery material that matched her eyes, with little chains for straps. As she shopped she thought about Dev, and about what he'd told her in the Mapparium. It was the first time a man had called her sexy, and when she closed her eyes she could still feel his whisper drifting through her body, under her skin. In the fitting room, which was just one big room with mirrors on the walls, she found a spot next to an older woman with a shiny face and coarse frosted hair. The woman stood barefoot in her underwear, pulling the black net of a body stocking taut between her fingers.

"Always check for snags," the woman advised.

Miranda pulled out the satin slip with scalloped edges. She held it to her chest.

The woman nodded with approval. "Oh yes."

"And this?" She held up the silver cocktail dress.

"Absolutely," the woman said. "He'll want to rip it right off you."

Miranda pictured the two of them at a restaurant in the South

** **mistress** *Geliebte*
buckle *Schnalle*
scalloped decorated with a row of curves

rack here: *Kleiderständer*

coarse rough; here: *widerspenstig*
taut stretched tight

snag small damaged area

South End trendy Boston neighbourhood

End they'd been to, where Dev had ordered foie gras and a soup made with champagne and raspberries. She pictured herself in the cocktail dress, and Dev in one of his suits, kissing her hand across the table. Only the next time Dev came to visit her, on a Sunday afternoon several days since the last time they'd seen each other, he was in gym clothes. After his wife came back, that was his excuse: on Sundays he drove into Boston and went running along the Charles. The first Sunday she opened the door in the knee-length robe, but Dev didn't even notice it; he carried her over to the bed, wearing sweatpants and sneakers, and entered her without a word. Later, she slipped on the robe when she walked across the room to get him a saucer for his cigarette ashes, but he complained that she was depriving him of the sight of her long legs, and demanded that she remove it. So the next Sunday she didn't bother. She wore jeans. She kept the lingerie at the back of a drawer, behind her socks and everyday underwear. The silver cocktail dress hung in her closet, the tag dangling from the seam. Often, in the morning, the dress would be in a heap on the floor; the chain straps always slipped off the metal hanger. Still, Miranda looked forward to Sundays. In the mornings she went to a deli and bought a baguette and little containers of things Dev liked to eat, like pickled herring, and potato salad, and tortes of pesto and mascarpone cheese. They ate in bed, picking up the herring with their fingers and ripping the baguette with their hands. Dev told her stories about his childhood, when he would come home from school and drink mango juice served to him on a tray, and then play cricket by a lake, dressed all in white. He told her about how, at eighteen, he'd been sent to a college in upstate New York during something called the Emergency, and about how it took him years to be able to follow American accents in movies, in spite of the fact that he'd had an English-medium education. As he talked he smoked three cigarettes, crushing them in a saucer by the side of her bed. Sometimes he asked her questions, like how many lovers she'd had (three) and how old she'd been the first time (nineteen). After lunch they made love, on sheets covered with crumbs, and then Dev took a nap for twelve minutes. Miranda had never known an adult who took naps, but Dev said it was something he'd grown up doing in India, where it was so hot that people didn't leave their homes until the sun went down. "Plus it allows us to sleep together," he murmured mischievously, curving his arm like a big bracelet around her body.

Only Miranda never slept. She watched the clock on her bedside table, or pressed her face against Dev's fingers, intertwined with hers, each with its half-dozen hairs at the knuckle. After six minutes she turned to face him, sighing and stretching, to test if he was really sleeping. He always was. His ribs were visible through his skin as he breathed, and yet he was beginning to develop a paunch. He complained about the hair on his shoulders, but Miranda thought him perfect, and refused to imagine him any other way.

At the end of twelve minutes Dev would open his eyes as if he'd been awake all along, smiling at her, full of a contentment she wished she felt herself. "The best twelve minutes of the week." He'd sigh, running a hand along the backs of her calves. Then he'd spring out of bed, pulling on his sweatpants and lacing up his sneakers. He would go to the bathroom and brush his teeth with his index finger, something he told her all Indians knew how to do, to get rid of the smoke in his mouth. When she kissed him good-bye she smelled herself sometimes in his hair. But she knew that his excuse, that he'd spent the afternoon jogging, allowed him to take a shower when he got home, first thing.

Apart from Laxmi and Dev, the only Indians Miranda had known were a family in the neighborhood where she'd grown up, named the Dixits. Much to the amusement of the neighborhood children, including Miranda, but not including the Dixit children, Mr. Dixit would jog each evening along the flat winding streets of their development in his everyday shirt and trousers, his only concession to athletic apparel being a pair of cheap Keds. Every weekend, the family — mother, father, two boys, and a girl — piled into their car and went away, to where nobody knew. The fathers complained that Mr. Dixit did not fertilize his lawn properly, did not rake his leaves on time, and agreed that the Dixit's house, the only one with vinyl siding, detracted from the neighborhood's charm. The mothers never invited Mrs. Dixit to join them around the Armstrongs' swimming pool. Waiting for the school bus with the Dixit children standing to one side, the other children would say "The Dixits dig shit," under their breath, and then burst into laughter.

One year, all the neighborhood children were invited to the birthday party of the Dixit girl. Miranda remembered an aroma of incense and onions in the house, and a pile of shoes heaped by the front door. But most of all she remembered a piece of fabric, about the size of a pillowcase, which hung from a wooden dowel at the bottom of the stairs. It was a painting of a naked woman with a red face shaped like a

paunch fat belly

calf, calves (pl.) *Wade*

Keds (brand name) American shoes

★**fabric** cloth, textile; underlying structure

knight's shield. She had enormous white eyes that tilted toward her temples, and mere dots for pupils. Two circles, with the same dots at their centers, indicated her breasts. In one hand she brandished a dagger. With one foot she crushed a struggling man on the ground. Around her body was a necklace composed of bleeding heads, strung together like a popcorn chain. She stuck her tongue out at Miranda.

"It is the goddess Kali," Mrs. Dixit explained brightly, shifting the dowel slightly in order to straighten the image. Mrs. Dixit's hands were painted with henna, an intricate pattern of zigzags and stars. "Come please, time for cake."

Miranda, then nine years old, had been too frightened to eat the cake. For months afterward she'd been too frightened even to walk on the same side of the street as the Dixits' house, which she had to pass twice daily, once to get to the bus stop, and once again go come home. For a while she even held her breath until she reached the next lawn, just as she did when the school bus passed a cemetery.

It shamed her now. Now, when she and Dev made love, Miranda closed her eyes and saw deserts and elephants, and marble pavilions floating on lakes beneath a full moon. One Saturday, having nothing else to do, she walked to Central Square, to an Indian restaurant, and ordered a plate of tandoori chicken. As she ate she tried to memorize phrases printed at the bottom of the menu, for things like "delicious" and "water" and "check, please." The phrases didn't stick in her mind, and so she began to stop from time to time in the foreign-language section of a bookstore in Kenmore Square, where she studied the Bengali alphabet in the Teach Yourself series. Once she went so far as to try to transcribe the Indian part of her name, "Mira," into her Filofax, her hand moving in unfamiliar directions, stopping and turning and picking up her pen when she least expected to. Following the arrows in the book, she drew a bar from left to right from which the letters hung; one looked more like a number than a letter, another looked like a triangle on its side. It had taken her several tries to get the letters of her name to resemble the sample letters in the book, and even then she wasn't sure if she'd written Mira or Mara. It was a scribble to her, but somewhere in the world, she realized with a shock, it meant something.

During the week it wasn't so bad. Work kept her busy, and she and Laxmi had begun having lunch together at a new Indian restaurant around the corner, during which Laxmi reported the latest status of her cousin's marriage. Sometimes Miranda tried to change the topic; it made her feel the way she once felt in college, when she and her boyfriend at the time had walked away from a crowded house of pancakes without paying for their food, just to see if they could get away with it. But Laxmi spoke of nothing else. "If I were her I'd fly straight to London and shoot them both," she announced one day. She snapped a papadum in half and dipped it into chutney. "I don't know how she can just wait this way."

Miranda knew how to wait. In the evenings she sat at her dining table and coated her nails with clear nail polish, and ate salad straight form the salad bowl, and watched television, and waited for Sunday. Saturdays were the worst because by Saturday it seemed that Sunday would never come. One Saturday when Dev called, late at night, she heard people laughing and talking in the background, so many that she asked him if he was at a concert hall. But he was only calling from his house in the suburbs. "I can't hear you that well," he said. "We have guests. Miss me?" She looked at the television screen, a sitcom that she'd muted with the remote control when the phone rang. She pictured him whispering into his cell phone, in a room upstairs, a hand on the doorknob, the hallway filled with guests. "Miranda, do you miss me?" he asked again. She told him that she did.

The next day, when Dev came to visit, Miranda asked him what his wife looked like. She was nervous to ask, waiting until he'd smoked the last of his cigarettes, crushing it with a firm twist into the saucer. She wondered if they'd quarrel. But Dev wasn't surprised by the question. He told her, spreading some smoked whitefish on a cracker, that his wife resembled an actress in Bombay named Madhuri Dixit.

For an instant Miranda's heart stopped. But no, the Dixit girl had been named something else, something that began with P. Still, she wondered if the actress and the Dixit girl were related. She'd been plain, wearing her hair in two braids all through high school.

A few days later Miranda went to an Indian grocery in Central Square which also rented videos. The door opened to a complicated tinkling of bells. It was dinnertime, and she was the only customer. A video was playing on a television hooked up in a corner of the store: a row of young women in harem pants were thrusting their hips in synchrony on a beach.

"Can I help you?" the man standing at the cash register asked. He was eating a samosa, dipping it into some dark brown sauce on a paper plate. Below the glass counter at his waist were trays of more plump samosas, and what looked like pale,

papadum thin, crisp, disc-shaped Indian food made from flour

to mute to turn off the sound, such as on TV

★ **to quarrel** to have an argument

braid (AE) *Zopf*

★ **to thrust** to move with a quick hard push

samosa fried or baked dish, often with a spicy filling

diamond-shaped pieces of fudge covered with foil, and some bright orange pastries floating in syrup. "You like some video?"

Miranda opened up her Filofax, where she had written down "Mottery Dixit." She looked up at the videos on the shelves behind the counter. She saw women wearing skirts that sat low on the hips and tops that tied like bandannas between their breasts. Some leaned back against a stone wall, or a tree. They were beautiful, the way the women dancing on the beach were beautiful, with kohl-rimmed eyes and long black hair. She knew then that Madhuri Dixit was beautiful, too.

"We have subtitled versions, miss," the man continued. He wiped his fingertips quickly on his shirt and pulled out three titles.

"No," Miranda said. "Thank you, no." She wandered through the store, studying shelves lined with unlabeled packets and tins. The freezer case was stuffed with bags of pita bread and vegetables she didn't recognize. The only thing she recognized was a rack lined with bags and bags of the Hot Mix that Laxmi was always eating. She thought about buying some for Laxmi, then hesitated, wondering how to explain what she'd been doing in an Indian grocery.

"Very spicy," the man said, shaking his head, his eyes travelling across Miranda's body. "Too spicy for you."

By February, Laxmi's cousin's husband still hadn't come to his senses. He had returned to Montreal, argued bitterly with his wife for two weeks, packed two suitcases, and flown back to London. He wanted a divorce.

Miranda sat in her cubicle and listened as Laxmi kept telling her cousin that there were better men in the world, just waiting to come out of the woodwork. The next day the cousin said she and her son were going to her parents' house in California, to try to recuperate. Laxmi convinced her to arrange a weekend layover in Boston. "A quick change of place will do you good," Laxmi insisted gently, "besides which, I haven't seen you in years."

Miranda stared at her own phone, wishing Dev would call. It had been four days since their last conversation. She heard Laxmi dialling directory assistance, asking for the number of a beauty salon. "Something soothing," Laxmi requested. She scheduled massages, facials, manicures, and pedicures. Then she reserved a table for lunch at the Four Seasons. In her determination to cheer up her cousin, Laxmi had forgotten about the boy. She rapped her knuckles on the laminated wall.

"Are you busy Saturday?"

The boy was thin. He wore a yellow knapsack strapped across his back, gray herringbone trousers, a red V-necked sweater, and black leather shoes. His hair was cut in a thick fringe over his eyes, which had dark circles under them. They were the first thing Miranda noticed. They made him look haggard, as if he smoked a great deal and slept very little, in spite of the fact that he was only seven years old. He clasped a large sketch pad with a spiral binding. His name was Rohin.

"Ask me a capital," he said, staring up at Miranda.

She stared back at him. It was eight-thirty on a Saturday morning. She took a sip of coffee. "A what?"

"It's a game he's been playing," Laxmi's cousin explained. She was thin like her son, with a long face and the same dark circles under her eyes. A rust-colored coat hung heavy on her shoulders. Her black hair, with a few strands of gray at the temples, was pulled back like a ballerina's. "You ask him a country and he tells you the capital."

"You should have heard him in the car," Laxmi said. "He's already memorized all of Europe."

"It's not a game," Rohin said. "I'm having a competition with a boy at school. We're competing to memorize all the capitals. I'm going to beat him."

Miranda nodded. "Okay. What's the capital of India?"

"That's no good." He marched away, his arms swinging like a toy soldier. Then he marched back to Laxmi's cousin and tugged at a pocket of her overcoat. "Ask me a hard one."

"Senegal," she said.

"Dakar!" Rohin exclaimed triumphantly, and began running in larger and larger circles. Eventually he ran into the kitchen. Miranda could hear him opening and closing the fridge.

"Rohin, don't touch without asking," Laxmi's cousin called out wearily. She managed a smile for Miranda. "Don't worry, he'll fall asleep in a few hours. And thanks for watching him."

"Back at three," Laxmi said, disappearing with her cousin down the hallway. "We're double-parked."

Miranda fastened the chain on the door. She went to the kitchen to find Rohin, but he was now in the living room, at the dining table, kneeling on one of the director's chairs. He unzipped his knapsack, pushed Miranda's basket of manicure supplies to one side of the table, and spread his crayons over the surface. Miranda stood over his shoulder. She watched as he gripped a blue crayon and drew the outline of an airplane.

"It's lovely," she said. When he didn't reply, she went to the kitchen to pour herself more coffee.

"Some for me, please," Rohin called out.

She returned to the living room. "Some what?"
"Some coffee. There's enough in the pot. I saw."
She walked over to the table and sat opposite him. At times he nearly stood up to reach for a new crayon. He barely made a dent in the director's chair.
"You're too young for coffee."
Rohin leaned over the sketch pad, so that his tiny chest and shoulders almost touched it, his head tilted to one side. "The stewardess let me have coffee," he said. "She made it with milk and lots of sugar." He straightened, revealing a woman's face beside the plane, with long wavy hair and eyes like asterisks. "Her hair was more shiny," he decided, adding, "My father met a pretty woman on a plane, too." He looked at Miranda. His face darkened as he watched her sip. "Can't I have just a little coffee? Please?"
She wondered, in spite of his composed brooding expression, if he were the type to throw a tantrum. She imagined his kicking her with his leather shoes, screaming for coffee, screaming and crying until his mother and Laxmi came back to fetch him. She went to the kitchen and prepared a cup for him as he'd requested. She selected a mug she didn't care for, in case he dropped it.
"Thank you," he said when she put it on the table. He took short sips, holding the mug securely with both hands.
Miranda sat with him while he drew, but when she attempted to put a coat of clear polish on her nails he protested. Instead he pulled out a paperback world almanac from his knapsack and asked her to quiz him. The countries were arranged by continent, six to a page, with the capitals in boldface, followed by a short entry on the population, government, and other statistics. Miranda turned to the middle of the Africa section and went down the list.
"Mali," she asked him.
"Bamako," he replied instantly.
"Malawi."
"Lilongwe."
She remembered looking at Africa in the Mapparium. She remembered the fat part of it was green.
"Go on," Rohin said.
"Mauritania."
"Nouakchott."
"Mauritius."
He paused, squeezed his eyes shut, then opened them, defeated. "I can't remember."
"Port Louis," she told him.

"Port Louis." He began to say it again and again, like a chant under his breath.

When they reached the last of the countries in Africa, Rohin said he wanted to watch cartoons, telling Miranda to watch them with him. When the cartoons ended, he followed her to the kitchen, and stood by her side as she made more coffee. He didn't follow her when she went to the bathroom a few minutes later, but when she opened the door she was startled to find him standing outside.

"Do you need to go?"

He shook his head but walked into the bathroom anyway. He put the cover of the toilet down, climbed on top of it, and surveyed the narrow glass shelf over the sink that held Miranda's toothbrush and makeup.

"What's this for?" he asked, picking up the sample of eye gel she'd got the day she met Dev.

"Puffiness."

"What's puffiness?"

"Here," she explained, pointing.

"After you've been crying?"

"I guess so."

Rohin opened the tube and smelled it. He squeezed a drop of it onto a finger, then rubbed it on his hand. "It stings." He inspected the back of his hand closely, as if expecting it to change color. "My mother has puffiness. She says it's a cold, but really she cries, sometimes for hours. Sometimes straight through dinner. Sometimes she cries so hard her eyes puff up like bullfrogs."

Miranda wondered if she ought to feed him. In the kitchen she discovered a bag of rice cakes and some lettuce. She offered to go out, to buy something from the deli, but Rohin said he wasn't very hungry, and accepted one of the rice cakes. "You eat one too," he said. They sat at the table, the rice cakes between them. He turned to a fresh page in his sketch pad. "You draw."

She selected a crayon. "What should I draw?"

He thought for a moment. "I know," he said. He asked her to draw things in the living room: the sofa, the director's chairs, the television, the telephone. "This way I can memorize it."

"Memorize what?"

"Our day together." He reached for another rice cake.

"Why do you want to memorize it?"

"Because we're never going to see each other, ever again."

The precision of the phrase startled her. She looked at him, feeling slightly depressed. Rohin didn't look depressed. He tapped the page. "Go on."

---

startled *suddenly surprised or frightened by sth*

puffiness *Aufgedunsenheit*

to sting *here: brennen*

And so she drew the items as best as she could — the sofa, the director's chairs, the television, the telephone. He sidled up to her, so close that it was sometimes difficult to see what she was doing. He put his small brown hand over hers. "Now me."
She handed him the crayon.
He shook his head. "No, now draw me."
"I can't", she said. "It won't look like you."
The brooding look began to spread across Rohin's face again, just as it had when she'd refused him coffee. "Please?"
She drew his face, outlining his head and the thick fringe of hair. He sat perfectly still, with a formal, melancholy expression, his gaze fixed to one side. Miranda wished she could draw a good likeness. Her hand moved in conjunction with her eyes, in unknown ways, just as it had that day in the bookstore when she'd transcribed her name in Bengali letters. It looked nothing like him. She was in the middle of drawing his nose when he wriggled away from the table.
"I'm bored," he announced, heading toward her bedroom. She heard him opening the door, opening the drawers of her bureau and closing them.
When she joined him he was inside the closet. He emerged, his hair dishevelled, holding the silver cocktail dress. "This was on the floor."
"It falls off the hanger."
Rohin looked at the dress and then at Miranda's body. "Put it on."
"Excuse me?"
"Put it on."
There was no reason to put it on. Apart from in the fitting room at Filene's she had never worn it, and as long as she was with Dev she knew she never would. She knew they would never go to restaurants, where he would reach across a table and kiss her hand. They would meet in her apartment, on Sundays, he in his sweatpants, she in her jeans. She took the dress from Rohin and shook it out, even though the slinky fabric never wrinkled. She reached into the closet for a free hanger.
"Please put it on," Rohin asked, suddenly standing behind her. He pressed his face against her, clasping her waist with both his thin arms. "Please?"
"All right," she said, surprised by the strength of his grip.
He smiled, satisfied, and sat on the edge of her bed.
"You have to wait out there," she said, pointing to the door. "I'll come out when I'm ready."
"But my mother always takes her clothes off in front of me."
"She does?"
Rohin nodded. "She doesn't even pick them up afterward. She

brooding serious, worried

leaves them all on the floor by the bed, all tangled."

"One day she slept in my room," he continued. "She said it felt better than her bed, now that my father's gone."

"I'm not your mother," Miranda said, lifting him by the armpits off her bed. When he refused to stand, she picked him up. He was heavier than she expected, and he clung to her, his legs wrapped firmly around her hips, his head resting against her chest. She set him down in the hallway and shut the door. As an extra precaution she fastened the latch. She changed into the dress, glancing into the full-length mirror nailed to the back of the door. Her ankle socks looked silly, and so she opened a drawer and found the stockings. She searched through the back of the closet and slipped on the high heels with the tiny buckles. The chain straps of the dress were as light as paper clips against her collarbone. It was a bit loose on her. She could not zip it herself.

Rohin began knocking. "May I come in now?"

She opened the door. Rohin was holding his almanac in his hands, muttering something under his breath. His eyes opened wide at the sight of her. "I need help with the zipper," she said. She sat on the edge of the bed.

Rohin fastened the zipper to the top, and then Miranda stood up and twirled. Rohin put down the almanac. "You're sexy," he declared.

"What did you say?"

"You're sexy."

Miranda sat down again. Though she knew it meant nothing, her heart skipped a beat. Rohin probably referred to all women as sexy. He'd probably heard the word on television, or seen it on the cover of a magazine. She remembered the day in the Mapparium, standing across the bridge from Dev. At the time she thought she knew what his words meant. At the time they'd made sense.

Miranda folded her arms across her chest and looked Rohin in the eyes. "Tell me something."

He was silent.

"What does it mean?"

"What?"

"That word. 'Sexy.' What does it mean?"

He looked down, suddenly shy. "I can't tell you."

"Why not?"

"It's a secret." He pressed his lips together, so hard that a bit of them went white.

"Tell me the secret. I want to know."

Rohin sat on the bed beside Miranda and began to kick the

edge of the mattress with the backs of his shoes. He giggled nervously, his thin body flinching as if it were being tickled.

"Tell me," Miranda demanded. She leaned over and gripped his ankles, holding his feet still.

Rohin looked at her, his eyes like slits. He struggled to kick the matress again, but Miranda pressed against him. He fell back on the bed, his back straight as a board. He cupped his hands around his mouth, and then he whispered, "It means loving someone you don't know."

Miranda felt Rohin's words under her skin, the same way she'd felt Dev's. But instead of going hot she felt numb. It reminded her of the way she'd felt at the Indian grocery, the moment she knew, without even looking at a picture, that Madhuri Dixit, whom Dev's wife resembled, was beautiful.

"That's what my father did," Rohin continued. "He sat next to someone he didn't know, someone sexy, and now he loves her instead of my mother."

He took off his shoes and placed them side by side on the floor. Then he peeled back the comforter and crawled into Miranda's bed with the almanac. A minute later the book dropped from his hands, and he closed his eyes. Miranda watched him sleep, the comforter rising and falling as he breathed. He didn't wake up after twelve minutes like Dev, or even twenty. He didn't open his eyes as she stepped out of the silver cocktail dress and back into her jeans, and put the high-heeled shoes in the back of the closet, and rolled up the stockings and put them back in her drawer.

When she had put everything away she sat on the bed again. She leaned toward him, close enough to see some white powder from the rice cakes stuck to the corners of his mouth, and picked up the almanac. As she turned the pages, she imagined the quarrels Rohin had overheard in his house in Montreal. "Is she pretty?" his mother would have asked his father, wearing the same bathrobe she'd worn for weeks, her own pretty face turning spiteful. "Is she sexy?" His father would deny it at first, try to change the subject. "Tell me," Rohin's mother would shriek, "tell me if she's sexy." In the end his father would admit that she was, and his mother would cry and cry, in a bed surrounded by a tangle of clothes, her eyes puffing up like bullfrogs. "How could you," she'd ask, sobbing, "how could you love a woman you don't even know?"

As Miranda imagined the scene she began to cry a little herself. In the Mapparium that day, all the countries had seemed close enough to touch, and Dev's voice had bounced wildly off the glass. From across the bridge, thirty feet away, his words had reached her ears, so near and full of warmth that they'd drifted for days under her skin. Miranda cried harder, unable to stop. But Rohin still slept. She guessed that he was used to it now, to the sound of a woman crying.

On Sunday, Dev called to tell Miranda he was on his way. "I'm almost ready. I'll be there at two."
She was watching a cooking show on television. A woman pointed to a row of apples, explaining which were best for baking. "You shouldn't come today."
"Why not?"
"I have a cold," she lied. It wasn't far from the truth; crying had left her congested. "I've been in bed all morning."
"You do sound stuffed up." There was a pause. "Do you need anything?"
"I'm all set."
"Drink lots of fluids."
"Dev?"
"Yes, Miranda?"
"Do you remember that day we went to the Mapparium?"
"Of course."
"Do you remember how we whispered to each other?"
"I remember," Dev whispered playfully.
"Do you remember what you said?"
There was a pause. " 'Let's go back to your place.' " He laughed quietly. "Next Sunday, then?"
The day before, as she'd cried, Miranda had believed she would never forget anything not even the way her name looked written in Bengali. She'd fallen asleep beside Rohin and when she woke up he was drawing an airplane on the copy of *The Economist* she'd saved, hidden under the bed. "Who's Devajit Mitra?" he had asked, looking at the address label.
Miranda pictured Dev, in his sweatpants and sneakers, laughing into the phone. In a moment he'd join his wife downstairs, and tell her he wasn't going jogging. He'd pulled a muscle while stretching, he'd say, settling down to read the paper. In spite of herself, she longed for him. She would see him one more Sunday, she decided, perhaps two. Then she would tell him the things she had known all along: that it wasn't fair to her, or to his wife, that they both deserved better, that there was no point in it dragging on.
But the next Sunday it snowed, so much so that Dev couldn't tell his wife he was going running along the Charles. The Sunday after that, the snow had melted, but Miranda made plans to go to the movies with Laxmi, and when she told Dev this

congested here: *verschnupft*

to drag on to continue for longer than you want

over the phone, he didn't ask her to cancel them. The third Sunday she got up early and went out for a walk. It was cold but sunny, and so she walked all the way down Commonwealth Avenue, past the restaurants where Dev had kissed her, and then she walked all the way to the Christian Science center. The Mapparium was closed, but she bought a cup of coffee nearby and sat on one of the benches in the plaza outside the church, gazing at its giant pillars and its massive dome, and at the clear-blue sky spread over the city.

The Norton Anthology of American Literature Vol. 2: 1865 to the Present. Eds. Nina Baym et al. Shorter 8th ed. New York: Norton, 2013, pp. 1650–1665.

Nilda
Junot Díaz

Nilda was my brother's girlfriend.
This is how all these stories begin.
She was Dominican from here and had super-long hair, like those Pentecostal girls, and a chest you wouldn't believe —
I'm talking world-class. Rafa would sneak her down into our basement bedroom after our mother went to bed and do her to whatever was on the radio right then. The two of them had to let me stay, because if my mother heard me upstairs on the couch everybody's ass would have been fried. And since I wasn't about to spend my night out in the bushes this is how it was.
Rafa didn't make no noise, just a low something that resembled breathing. Nilda was the one. She seemed to be trying to hold back from crying the whole time. It was crazy hearing her like that. The Nilda I'd grown up with was one of the quietest girls you'd ever meet. She let her hair wall away her face and read *The New Mutants*, and the only time she looked straight at anything was when she looked out a window.
But that was before she'd gotten that chest, before that slash of black hair had gone from something to pull on the bus to something to stroke in the dark. The new Nilda wore stretch pants and Iron Maiden shirts; she had already run away from her mother's and ended up at a group home; she'd already slept with Toño and Nestor and Little Anthony from Parkwood, older guys. She crashed over at our apartment a lot because she hated her moms, who was the neighborhood borracha. In the morning she slipped out before my mother woke up and found her. Waited for heads at the bus stop, fronted like she'd come from her own place, same clothes as the day before and greasy hair so everybody thought her a skank. Waited for my brother and didn't talk to anybody and nobody talked to her, because she'd always been one of those quiet, semi-retarded girls who you couldn't talk to without being dragged into a whirlpool of dumb stories. If Rafa decided that he wasn't going to school, then she'd wait near our apartment until my mother left for work. Sometimes Rafa let her in right away. Sometimes he slept late and she'd wait across the street, building letters out of pebbles until she saw him crossing the living room.
She had big stupid lips and a sad moonface and the driest skin. Always rubbing lotion on it and cursing the moreno father who'd given it to her.

⬅ What kind of narrator do you expect?

Pentecostal belonging to Pentecostalism, a movement within Protestant Christianity; *Pfingstbewegung*

New Jersey
Population: 8.9 million; area: 22,591 km²; capital: Trenton; nickname: Garden State; abbreviation: NJ.
Many of Díaz's short stories are set in towns and neighbourhoods of Middlesex County, NJ. Locations mentioned in "Nilda" include Parkwood, South Amboy, Sayreville, Amsterdam Village and London Terrace. The city of New Brunswick, which is home to Rutgers University, is located in this county.

The New Mutants an American comic book series
* to stroke to gently move your hand over skin, hair, or fur
Iron Maiden successful British heavy metal band founded in 1975
moms (infml.) mother
borracha (Sp.) female alcoholic

skank (pej.) a lower-class person with poor hygiene, perhaps a prostitute
retarded (pej.) mentally disabled

pebble *Kieselstein*

moreno, morena (Sp.) person of dark skin

It seemed like she was always waiting for my brother. Nights she'd knock and I'd let her in and we'd sit on the couch while Rafa was off at his job at the carpet factory or working out at the gym. I'd show her my newest comics and she'd read them real close, but as soon as Rafa showed up she'd throw them in my lap and jump into his arms. I missed you, she'd say in a little-girl voice, and Rafa would laugh. You should have seen him in those days: he had the face bones of a saint. Then Mami's door would open and Rafa would detach himself and cowboy-saunter over to Mami and say, You got something for me to eat, vieja? Claro que sí, Mami'd say, trying to put her glasses on.

He had us all, the way only a pretty nigger can.

Once when Rafa was late from the job and we were alone in the apartment a long time, I asked her about the group home. It was three weeks before the end of the school year and everybody had entered the Do-Nothing Stage. I was fourteen and reading *Dhalgren* for the second time; I had an IQ that would have broken you in two but I would have traded it in for a halfway decent face in a second.

It was pretty cool up there, she said. She was pulling on the front of her halter top, trying to air her chest out. The food was *bad* but there were a lot of cute guys in the house with me. They *all* wanted me.

She started chewing on a nail. Even the guys who worked there were calling me after I left, she said.

The only reason Rafa went after her was because his last full-time girlfriend had gone back to Guyana — she was this dougla girl with a single eyebrow and skin to die for — and because Nilda had pushed up to him. She'd only been back from the group home a couple of months, but by then she'd already gotten a rep as a cuero. A lot of the Dominican girls in town were on some serious lockdown — we saw them on the bus and at school and maybe at the Pathmark, but since most families knew exactly what kind of tigueres were roaming the neighborhood these girls weren't allowed to hang out. Nilda was different. She was brown trash. Her moms was a mean-ass drunk and always running around South Amboy with her white boyfriends — which is a long way of saying Nilda could hang and, man, did she ever. Always out in the world, always cars stopping where she was smoking cigarettes. Before I even knew she was back from the group home she got scooped up by this older nigger from the back apartments. He kept her on his dick for almost four months, and I used to see them driving around in his fucked-up rust-eaten Sunbird while I delivered my papers. Motherfucker was like three hundred years old, but because he had a car and a record collection and foto albums from his Vietnam days and because he bought her clothes to replace the old shit she was wearing, Nilda was all lost on him.

I hated this nigger with a passion, but when it came to guys there was no talking to Nilda. I used to ask her, What's up with Wrinkle Dick? And she would get so mad she wouldn't speak to me for days, and then I'd get this note, *I want you to respect my man.* Whatever, I'd write back. Then the old cat bounced, no one knew where, the usual scenario in my neighborhood, and for a couple of months she got tossed by those cats from Parkwood. On Thursdays, which was comic-book day, she'd drop in to see what I'd picked up and she'd talk to me about how unhappy she was. We'd sit together until it got dark and then her beeper would fire up and she'd peer into its display and say, I have to go. Sometimes I could grab her and pull her back on the couch, and we'd stay there a long time, me waiting for her to fall in love with me, her waiting for whatever, but other times she'd be serious. I have to go see my man, she'd say.

One of those comic-book days she saw my brother coming back from his five-mile run. Rafa was still boxing then and he was cut up like crazy, the muscles on his chest and abdomen so striated they looked like something out of a Frazetta drawing. He noticed her because she was wearing these ridiculous shorts and this tank that couldn't have blocked a sneeze and a thin roll of stomach was poking from between the fabrics and he smiled at her and she got real serious and uncomfortable and he told her to fix him some iced tea and she told him to fix it himself. You a guest here, he said. You should be earning your fucking keep. He went into the shower and as soon as he did she was in the kitchen stirring and I told her to leave it, but she said, I might as well. We drank all of it.

I wanted to warn her, tell her he was a monster, but she was already headed for him at the speed of light.

The next day Rafa's car turned up broken — what a coincidence — so he took the bus to school and when he was walking past our seat he took her hand and pulled her to her feet and she said, Get off me. Her eyes were pointed straight at the floor. I just want to show you something, he said. She was pulling with her arm but the rest of her was ready to go. Come on, Rafa said, and finally she went. Save my seat, she said over her shoulder, and I was like, Don't worry about it. Before we even swung onto 516 Nilda was in my brother's lap and he had his hand so far up her skirt it looked like he was performing a surgical procedure. When we were getting off the bus Rafa pulled me aside and held his hand in front of my nose. Smell this, he said. This, he said, is what's wrong with women.

You couldn't get anywhere near Nilda for the rest of the day. She had her hair pulled back and was glorious with victory. Even the white girls knew about my overmuscled about-to-be-a-senior brother and were impressed. And while Nilda sat at the end of our lunch table and whispered to some girls me and my boys ate our crap sandwiches and talked about the X-Men — this was back when the X-Men still made some kind of sense — and even if we didn't want to admit it the truth was now patent and awful: all the real dope girls were headed up to the high school, like moths to a light, and there was nothing any of us younger cats could do about it. My man José Negrón — a.k.a. Joe Black — took Nilda's defection the hardest, since he'd actually imagined he had a chance with her. Right after she got back from the group home he'd held her hand on the bus, and even though she'd gone off with other guys, he'd never forgotten it. I was in the basement three nights later when they did it. That first time neither of them made a sound.

They went out that whole summer. I don't remember anyone doing anything big. Me and my pathetic little crew hiked over to Morgan Creek and swam around in water stinking of leachate from the landfill; we were just getting serious about the licks that year and Joe Black was stealing bottles out of his father's stash and we were drinking them down to the corners on the swings behind the apartments. Because of the heat and because of what I felt inside my chest a lot, I often just sat in the crib with my brother and Nilda. Rafa was tired all the time and pale: this had happened in a matter of days. I used to say, Look at you, white boy, and he used to say, Look at you, you black ugly nigger. He didn't feel like doing much, and besides his car had finally broken down for real, so we would all sit in the air-conditioned apartment and watch TV. Rafa had decided he wasn't going back to school for his senior year, and even though my moms was heartbroken and trying to guilt him into it five times a day, this was all he talked about. School had never been his gig, and after my pops left us for his twenty-five-year-old he didn't feel he needed to pretend any longer. I'd like to take a long fucking trip, he told us. See California before it slides into the ocean. California, I said. California, he said. A nigger could make a showing out there. I'd like to go there, too, Nilda said, but Rafa didn't answer her. He had closed his eyes and you could see he was in pain.

We never talked about our father. I'd asked Rafa once, right at the beginning of the Last Great Absence, where he thought he was, and Rafa said, Like I fucking care.

End of conversation. World without end.

On days niggers were really out of their minds with boredom we trooped down to the pool and got in for free because Rafa was boys with one of the lifeguards. I swam, Nilda went on missions around the pool just so she could show off how tight she looked in her bikini, and Rafa sprawled under the awning and took it all in. Sometimes he called me over and we'd sit together for a while and he'd close his eyes and I'd watch the water dry on my ashy legs and then he'd tell me to go back to the pool. When Nilda finished promenading and came back to where Rafa was chilling she kneeled at his side and he would kiss her real long, his hands playing up and down the length of her back. Ain't nothing like a fifteen-year-old with a banging body, those hands seemed to be saying, at least to me.

Joe Black was always watching them. Man, he muttered, she's so fine I'd lick her asshole *and* tell you niggers about it.

Maybe I would have thought they were cute if I hadn't known Rafa. He might have seemed enamora'o with Nilda but he also had mad girls in orbit. Like this one piece of white trash from Sayreville, and this morena from Amsterdam Village who also slept over and sounded like a freight train when they did it. I don't remember her name, but I do remember how her perm shone in the glow of our night-light.

In August Rafa quit his job at the carpet factory — I'm too fucking tired, he complained, and some mornings his leg bones hurt so much he couldn't get out of bed right away. The Romans used to shatter these with iron clubs, I told him while I massaged his shins. The pain would kill you instantly. Great, he said. Cheer me up some more, you fucking bastard. One day Mami took him to the hospital for a checkup and afterward I found them sitting on the couch, both of them dressed up, watching TV like nothing had happened. They were holding hands and Mami appeared tiny next to him.

Well?

Rafa shrugged. The doc thinks I'm anemic.

Anemic ain't bad.

Yeah, Rafa said, laughing bitterly. God bless Medicaid.

In the light of the TV, he looked terrible.

That was the summer when everything we would become

was hovering just over our heads. Girls were starting to take notice of me; I wasn't good-looking but I listened and was sincere and had boxing muscles in my arms. In another universe I probably came out O.K., ended up with mad novias and jobs and a sea of love in which to swim, but in this world I had a brother who was dying of cancer and a long dark patch of life like a mile of black ice waiting for me up ahead.

One night, a couple of weeks before school started — they must have thought I was asleep — Nilda started telling Rafa about her plans for the future. I think even she knew what was about to happen. Listening to her imagining herself was about the saddest thing you ever heard. How she wanted to get away from her moms and open up a group home for runaway kids. But this one would be real cool, she said. It would be for normal kids who just got problems. She must have loved him because she went on and on. Plenty of people talk about having a flow, but that night I really heard one, something that was unbroken, that fought itself and worked together all at once. Rafa didn't say nothing. Maybe he had his hands in her hair or maybe he was just like, Fuck you. When she finished he didn't even say wow. I wanted to kill myself with embarrassment. About a half hour later she got up and dressed. She couldn't see me or she would have known that I thought she was beautiful. She stepped into her pants and pulled them up in one motion, sucked in her stomach while she buttoned them. I'll see you later, she said.

Yeah, he said.

After she walked out he put on the radio and started on the speed bag. I stopped pretending I was asleep; I sat up and watched him.

Did you guys have a fight or something?

No, he said.

Why'd she leave?

He sat down on my bed. His chest was sweating. She had to go.

But where's she gonna stay?

I don't know. He put his hand on my face, gently. Why ain't you minding your business?

A week later he was seeing some other girl. She was from Trinidad, a coco pañyol, and she had this phony-as-hell English accent. It was the way we all were back then. None of us wanted to be niggers. Not for nothing.

I guess two years passed. My brother was gone by then, and I was on my way to becoming a nut. I was out of school most of the time and had no friends and I sat inside and watched Univisión or walked down to the dump and smoked the mota I should have been selling until I couldn't see. Nilda didn't fare so well, either. A lot of the things that happened to her, though, had nothing to do with me or my brother. She fell in love a couple more times, really bad with this one moreno truck driver who took her to Manalapan and then abandoned her at the end of the summer. I had to drive over to get her, and the house was one of those tiny box jobs with a fifty-cent lawn and no kind of charm; she was acting like she was some Italian chick and offered me a joint in the car, but I put my hand on hers and told her to stop it. Back home she fell in with more stupid niggers, relocated kids from the City, and they came at her with drama and some of their girls beat her up, a Brick City beat-down, and she lost her bottom front teeth. She was in and out of school and for a while they put her on home instruction, and that was when she finally dropped.

My junior year she started delivering papers so she could make money, and since I was spending a lot of time outside I saw her every now and then. Broke my heart. She wasn't at her lowest yet but she was aiming there and when we passed each other she always smiled and said hi. She was starting to put on weight and she'd cut her hair down to nothing and her moonface was heavy and alone. I always said Wassup and when I had cigarettes I gave them to her. She'd gone to the funeral, along with a couple of his other girls, and what a skirt she'd worn, like maybe she could still convince him of something, and she'd kissed my mother but the vieja hadn't known who she was. I had to tell Mami on the ride home and all she could remember about her was that she was the one who smelled good. It wasn't until Mami said it that I realized it was true.

It was only one summer and she was nobody special, so what's the point of all this? He's gone, he's gone, he's gone. I'm twenty-three and I'm washing my clothes up at the mini mall on Ernston Road. She's here with me — she's folding her shit and smiling and showing me her missing teeth and saying, It's been a long time, hasn't it, Yunior?

Years, I say, loading my whites. Outside the sky is clear of gulls, and down at the apartment my moms is waiting for me with dinner. Six months earlier we were sitting in front of the TV and my mother said, Well, I think I'm finally over this place.

Nilda asks, Did you move or something?

I shake my head. Just been working.

God, it's been a long, long time. She's on her clothes like magic, making everything neat, making everything fit. There are four other people at the counters, broke-ass-looking niggers with knee socks and croupier's hats and scars snaking up their arms, and they all seem like sleepwalkers compared with her. She shakes her head, grinning. Your brother, she says.

Rafa.

She points her finger at me like my brother always did.

I miss him sometimes.

She nods. Me, too. He was a good guy to me.

I must have disbelief on my face because she finishes shaking out her towels and then stares straight through me. He treated me the best.

Nilda.

He used to sleep with my hair over his face. He used to say it made him feel safe.

to stack *stapeln*

What else can we say? She finishes her stacking, I hold the door open for her. The locals watch us leave. We walk back through the old neighborhood, slowed down by the bulk of our clothes. London Terrace has changed now that the landfill has shut down. Kicked-up rents and mad South Asian people and white folks living in the apartments, but it's our kids you

porch (AE) veranda (BE)

see in the streets and hanging from the porches.

Nilda is watching the ground as though she's afraid she might fall. My heart is beating and I think, We could do anything. We could marry. We could drive off to the West Coast. We could start over. It's all possible but neither of us speaks for a long time and the moment closes and we're back in the world we've always known.

Remember the day we met? she asks.

I nod.

You wanted to play baseball.

It was summer, I say. You were wearing a tank top.

You made me put on a shirt before you'd let me be on your team. Do you remember?

I remember, I say.

We never spoke again. A couple of years later I went away to college and I don't know where the fuck she went.

The Scribner Anthology of Contemporary Short Fiction: 50 North America Short Stories since 1970. Eds. Lex Williford, Michael Martone. 2nd ed. New York: Touchstone, 2007, pp. 144–151.

Twilight of the Superheroes
Deborah Eisenberg

NATHANIEL RECALLS THE MIRACLE

The grandchildren approach.
Nathaniel can make them out dimly in the shadows. When it's time, he'll tell them about the miracle.
It was the dawn of the new millennium, he'll say. *I was living in the Midwest back then, but my friends from college persuaded me to come to New York.*
I arrived a few days ahead of the amazing occasion, and all over the city there was an atmosphere of feverish anticipation. The year two thousand! The new millennium! Some people thought it was sure to be the end of the world. Others thought we were at the threshold of something completely new and better. The tabloids carried wild predictions from celebrity clairvoyants, and even people who scoffed and said that the date was an arbitrary and meaningless one were secretly agitated. In short, we were suddenly aware of ourselves standing there, staring at the future blindfolded.
I suppose, looking back on it, that all the commotion seems comical and ridiculous. And perhaps you're thinking that we churned it up to entertain ourselves because we were bored or because our lives felt too easy — trivial and mundane. But consider: ceremonial occasions, even purely personal ones like birthdays or anniversaries, remind us that the world is full of terrifying surprises and no one knows what even the very next second will bring!
Well, shortly before the momentous day, a strange news item appeared: experts were saying that a little mistake had been made — just one tiny mistake, a little detail in the way computers everywhere had been programmed. But the consequences of this detail, the experts said, were potentially disastrous; tiny as it was, the detail might affect everybody, and in a very big way! You see, if history has anything to teach us, it's that — despite all our efforts, despite our best (or worst) intentions, despite our touchingly indestructible faith in our own foresight — we poor humans cannot actually think ahead; there are just too many variables. And so, when it comes down to it, it always turns out that no one is in charge of the things that really matter.
It must be hard for you to imagine — it's even hard for me to remember — but people hadn't been using computers for very long. As far as I know, my mother (your great-grandmother)

* threshold Schwelle
clairvoyant sb who claims to predict the future

blindfolded mit verbundenen Augen

mundane ordinary

never even touched one! And no one had thought to inform the computers that one day the universe would pass from the years of the one thousands into the years of the two thousands. So the machines, as these experts suddenly realized, were not equipped to understand that at the conclusion of 1999 time would not start over from 1900, time would keep going.

People all over America — all over the world! — began to speak of "a crisis of major proportions" (which was a phrase we used to use back then). Because, all the routine operations that we'd so blithely delegated to computers, the operations we all took for granted and depended on — how would they proceed?

Might one be fatally trapped in an elevator? Would we have to huddle together for warmth and scrabble frantically through our pockets for a pack of fancy restaurant matches so we could set our stacks of old New York Reviews ablaze? Would all the food rot in heaps out there on the highways, leaving us to pounce on fat old street rats and grill them over the flames? What was going to happen to our bank accounts — would they vaporize? And what about air traffic control? On December 31 when the second hand moved from 11:59:59 to midnight, would all the airplanes in the sky collide?

Everyone was thinking of more and more alarming possibilities. Some people committed their last night on this earth to partying, and others rushed around buying freeze-dried provisions and cases of water and flashlights and radios and heavy blankets in the event that the disastrous problem might somehow eventually be solved.

And then, as the clock ticked its way through the enormous gatherings in celebration of the era that was due to begin in a matter of hours, then minutes, then seconds, we waited to learn the terrible consequences of the tiny oversight. Khartoum, Budapest, Paris — we watched on television, our hearts fluttering, as midnight, first just a tiny speck in the east, unfurled gently, darkening the sky and moving toward us over the globe.

But the amazing thing, Nathaniel will tell his grandchildren, was that nothing happened! We held our breath ... And there was nothing! It was a miracle. Over the face of the earth, from east to west and back again, nothing catastrophic happened at all.

Oh, well. Frankly, by the time he or any of his friends get around to producing a grandchild (or even a child, come to think of it) they might well have to explain what computers had been. And freeze-dried food. And celebrity clairvoyants and airplanes and New York and America and even cities, and heaven only knows what.

---

blithely mindlessly, without thinking

stack here: pile of magazines
ablaze on fire
to pounce on sth *sich auf etw. stürzen*

FROGBOIL

Lucien watches absently as his assistant, Sharmila, prepares to close up the gallery for the evening; something keeps tugging at his attention …

Oh, yes. It's the phrase Yoshi Matsumoto used this morning when he called from Tokyo. *Back to normal … Back to normal …* What's that famous, revolting, sadistic experiment? Something like, you drop the frog into a pot of boiling water and it jumps out. But if you drop it into a pot of cold water and slowly bring the water to a boil, the frog stays put and gets boiled.

Itami Systems is reopening its New York branch, was what Matsumoto called to tell Lucien; he'll be returning to the city soon. Lucien pictured his old friend's mournful, ironic expression as he added, "They tell me they're 'exploring additional avenues of development now that New York is back to normal.'"

Lucien had made an inadvertent squawklike sound. He shook his head, then he shook his head again.

"Hello?" Matsumoto said.

"I'm here," Lucien said. "Well, it'll be good to see you again. But steel yourself for a wait at customs; they're fingerprinting."

inadvertent unintentional
to squawk to shriek

★ **customs** (pl.) *Zollbehörde*

VIEW

Mr. Matsumoto's loft is a jungle of big rubbery trees, under which crouch sleek items of chrome and leather. Spindly electronic devices blink or warble amid the foliage, and here and there one comes upon an immense flat-screen TV — the first of their kind that Nathaniel ever handled.

Nathaniel and his friends have been subletting — thanks, obviously, to Uncle Lucien — for a ridiculously minimal rent and on Mr. Matsumoto's highly tolerable conditions of cat-sitting and general upkeep. Nathaniel and Lyle and Amity and Madison each have something like an actual bedroom, and there are three whole bathrooms, one equipped with a Jacuzzi. The kitchen, stone and steel, has cupboards bigger than most of their friends' apartments. Art — important, soon to be important, or very recently important, most of which was acquired from Uncle Lucien — hangs on the walls.

And the terrace! One has only to open the magic sliding panel to find oneself halfway to heaven. On the evening, over three

to crouch *sich kauern*
sleek *elegant*

★ **to sublet** *zur Untermiete wohnen; untervermieten*

Jacuzzi (brand name) producer of whirlpool bathtubs

years ago, when Uncle Lucien completed the arrangements for Nathaniel to sublet and showed him the place, Nathaniel stepped out onto the terrace and tears shot right up into his eyes.

There was that unearthly palace, the Chrysler Building! There was the Empire State Building, like a brilliant violet hologram! There were the vast, twinkling prairies of Brooklyn and New Jersey! And best of all, Nathaniel could make out the Statue of Liberty holding her torch aloft, as she had held it for each of his parents when they arrived as children from across the ocean — terrified, filthy and hungry — to safety.

Stars glimmered nearby; towers and spires, glowing emerald, topaz, ruby, sapphire, soared below. The avenues and bridges slung a trembling net of light across the rivers, over the buildings. Everything was spangled and dancing; the little boats glittered. The lights floated up and up like bubbles.

Back when Nathaniel moved into Mr. Matsumoto's loft, shortly after his millennial arrival in New York, sitting out on the terrace had been like looking down over the rim into a gigantic glass of champagne.

UNCLE LUCIEN'S WORDS OF REASSURANCE

So, Matsumoto is returning. And Lucien has called Nathaniel, the nephew of his adored late wife, Charlie, to break the news. Well, of course it's hardly a catastrophe for the boy. Matsumoto's place was only a sublet in any case, and Nathaniel and his friends will all find other apartments.

But it's such an ordeal in this city. And all four of the young people, however different they might be, strike Lucien as being in some kind of holding pattern — as if they're temporizing, or muffled by unspoken reservations. Of course, he doesn't really know them. Maybe it's just the eternal, poignant weariness of youth.

The strangest thing about getting old (or one of the many strangest things) is that young people sometimes appear to Lucien — as, in fact, Sharmila does at this very moment — in a nimbus of tender light. It's as if her unrealized future were projecting outward like ectoplasm.

"Doing anything entertaining this evening?" he asks her.

She sighs. "Time will tell," she says.

She's a nice young woman; he'd like to give her a few words of advice, or reassurance.

But what could they possibly be? "Don't — " he begins.

Don't worry? HAHAHAHAHA! Don't feel *sad*? "Don't bother about the phones," is what he settles down on. A new show goes up tomorrow, and it's become Lucien's custom on such evenings to linger in the stripped gallery and have a glass of wine. "I'll take care of them."

But how has he *gotten* so old?

SUSPENSION

So, there was the famous, strangely blank New Year's Eve, the nothing at all that happened, neither the apocalypse nor the failure of the planet's computers, nor, evidently, the dawning of a better age. Nathaniel had gone to parties with his old friends from school and was asleep before dawn; the next afternoon he awoke with only a mild hangover and an uneasy impression of something left undone.

Next thing you knew, along came that slump, as it was called — the general economic blight that withered the New York branch of Mr. Matsumoto's firm and clusters of jobs all over the city. There appeared to be no jobs at all, in fact, but then — somehow — Uncle Lucien unearthed one for Nathaniel in the architectural division of the subway system. It was virtually impossible to afford an apartment, but Uncle Lucien arranged for Nathaniel to sublet Mr. Matsumoto's loft.

Then Madison and his girlfriend broke up, so Madison moved into Mr. Matsumoto's, too. Not long afterward, the brokerage house where Amity was working collapsed resoundingly, and she'd joined them. Then Lyle's landlord jacked up his rent, so Lyle started living at Mr. Matsumoto's as well.

As the return of Mr. Matsumoto to New York was contingent upon the return of a reasonable business climate, one way or another it had sort of slipped their minds that Mr. Matsumoto was real. And for over three years there they've been hanging in temporary splendor thirty-one floors above the pavement. They're all out on the terrace this evening. Madison has brought in champagne so that they can salute with an adequate flourish the end of their tenure in Mr. Matsumoto's place. And except for Amity, who takes a principled stand against thoughtful moods, and Amity's new friend or possibly suitor, Russell, who has no history here, they're kind of quiet.

slump economic or financial decline
to wither sth *etw. austrocknen lassen*

brokerage house place where a broker does his/her business; *Maklerbüro*

to be contingent upon sth to be dependent on sth

suitor (old) man who tries to date a woman

REUNION

Now that Sharmila has gone, Lucien's stunning, cutting-edge gallery space blurs a bit and recedes. The room, in fact, seems almost like an old snapshot from that bizarre, quaintly futuristic century, the twentieth. Lucien takes a bottle of white wine from the little fridge in the office, pours himself a glass, and from behind a door in that century emerges Charlie.

Charlie — Oh, how long it's been, how unbearably long! Lucien luxuriates in the little pulse of warmth just under his skin that indicates her presence. He strains for traces of her voice, but her words degrade like the words in a dream, as if they're being rubbed through a sieve.

Yes, yes, Lucien assures her. He'll put his mind to finding another apartment for her nephew. And when her poor, exasperating sister and brother-in-law call frantically about Nathaniel, as they're bound to do, he'll do his best to calm them down.

But what a nuisance it all is! The boy is as opaque to his parents as a turnip. He was the child of their old age and he's also, obviously, the repository of all of their baroque hopes and fears. By their own account, they throw up their hands and wring them, lecture Nathaniel about frugality, then press spending money upon him and fret when he doesn't use it.

Between Charlie's death and Nathaniel's arrival in New York, Lucien heard from Rose and Isaac only at what they considered moments of emergency: Nathaniel's grades were erratic! His friends were bizarre! Nathaniel had expressed an interest in architecture, an unreliable future! He drew, and Lucien had better sit down, *comics*!

The lamentations would pour through the phone, and then, the instant Lucien hung up, evaporate. But if he had given the matter one moment's thought, he realizes, he would have understood from very early on that it was only a matter of time until the boy found his way to the city.

It was about four years ago now that Rose and Isaac put in an especially urgent call. Lucien held the receiver at arm's length and gritted his teeth. "You're an important man," Rose was shouting. "We understand that, we understand how busy you are, you know we'd never do this, but it's an emergency. The boy's in New York, and he sounds terrible. He doesn't have a job, lord only knows what he eats — I don't know what to think, Lucien, he *drifts*, he's just *drifting*. Call him, promise me, that's all I'm asking."

"Fine, certainly, good," Lucien said, already gabbling; he would have agreed to anything if Rose would only hang up.

"But whatever you do," she added, "please, please, under no circumstances should you let him know that we asked you to call."

Lucien looked at the receiver incredulously. "But how else

would I have known he was in New York?" he said. "How else would I have gotten his number?"

There was a silence, and then a brief, amazed laugh from Isaac on another extension. "Well, I don't know what you'll tell him," Isaac said admiringly. "But you're the brains of the family, you'll think of something."

INNOCENCE

And actually, Russell (who seems to be not only Amity's friend and possible suitor but also her agent) has obtained for Amity a whopping big advance from some outfit that Madison refers to as Cheeseball Editions, so whatever else they might all be drinking to (or drinking about) naturally Amity's celebrating a bit. And Russell, recently arrived from L.A., cannot suppress his ecstasy about how *ur* New York, as he puts it, Mr. Matsumoto's loft is, tactless as he apparently recognizes this untimely ecstasy to be.

"It's *fantastic*," he says. "Who did it, do you know?"

Nathaniel nods. "Matthias Lehmann."

"That's what I thought, I thought so," Russell says. "It *looks* like Lehmann. Oh, wow, I can't believe you guys have to move out — I mean, it's just so totally amazing!"

Nathaniel and Madison nod and Lyle sniffs peevishly. Lyle is stretched out on a yoga mat that Nathaniel once bought in preparation for a romance (as yet manqué) with a prettily tattooed yoga teacher he runs into in the bodega on the corner. Lyle's skin has a waxy, bluish cast; there are dark patches beneath his eyes. He looks like a child too precociously worried to sleep. His boyfriend, Jahan, has more or less relocated to London, and Lyle has been missing him frantically. Lying there so still on the yoga mat with his eyes closed, he appears to be a tomb sculpture from an as yet nonexistent civilization.

"And the view!" Russell says. "This is probably the most incredible view on the *planet*."

The others consider the sight of Russell's eager face. And then Amity says, "More champagne, anyone?"

Well, sure, who knows where Russell had been? Who knows where he would have been on that shining, calm, perfectly blue September morning when the rest of them were here having coffee on the terrace and looked up at the annoying racket of a low-flying plane? Why should they expect Russell — now, nearly three years later — to imagine that moment out on the terrace when Lyle spilled his coffee and said, "Oh, shit," and something flashed and something tore, and the cloudless sky ignited.

HOME

Rose and Isaac have elbowed their way in behind Charlie, and no matter how forcefully Lucien tries to boot them out, they're making themselves at home, airing their dreary history.

Both sailed as tiny, traumatized children with their separate families and on separate voyages right into the Statue of Liberty's open arms. Rose was almost eleven when her little sister, Charlie, came into being, along with a stainless American birth certificate.

Neither Rose and Charlie's parents nor Isaac's ever recovered from their journey to the New World, to say nothing of what had preceded it. The two sets of old folks spoke, between them, Yiddish, Polish, Russian, German, Croatian, Slovenian, Ukrainian, Ruthenian, Rumanian, Latvian, Czech, and Hungarian, Charlie had once told Lucien, but not one of the four ever managed to learn more English than was needed to procure a quarter pound of smoked sturgeon from the deli. They worked impossible hours, they drank a little schnapps, and then, in due course, they died.

Isaac did fairly well manufacturing vacuum cleaners. He and Rose were solid members of their temple and the community, but, according to Charlie, no matter how uneventful their lives in the United States continued to be, filling out an unfamiliar form would cause Isaac's hands to sweat and send jets of acid through his innards. When he or Rose encountered someone in uniform — a train conductor, a meter maid, a crossing guard — their hearts would leap into their throats and they would think: *passport!*

Their three elder sons, Nathaniel's brothers, fulfilled Rose and Isaac's deepest hopes by turning out to be blindingly inconspicuous. The boys were so reliable and had so few characteristics it was hard to imagine what anyone could think up to kill them for. They were Jewish, of course, but even Rose and Isaac understood that this particular criterion was inoperative in the United States — at least for the time being.

The Old World, danger, and poverty were far in the past. Nevertheless, the family lived in their tidy, midwestern house with its two-car garage as if secret police were permanently hiding under the matching plastic-covered sofas, as if Brown-shirts and Cossacks were permanently rampaging through the suburban streets.

Lucien knew precious little about vacuum cleaners and nothing at all about childhood infections or lawn fertilizers. And

---

dreary depressing, gloomy

sturgeon *Stör*

innards (pl., infml.) organs inside the human body

inconspicuous hardly noticeable

Brown-shirts the Nazi Regime's *Sturmabteilung*
Cossacks semi-military communities located in the Ukraine and Russia

yet, as soon as Charlie introduced him, Isaac and Rose set about soliciting his views as if he were an authority on everything that existed on their shared continent.

His demurrals, disclaimers, and protestations of ignorance were completely ineffective. Whatever guess he was finally strong-armed into hazarding was received as oracular. Oracular!

Fervent gratitude was expressed: Thank God Charlie had brought Lucien into the family! How brilliant he was, how knowledgeable and subtle! And then Rose and Isaac would proceed to pick over his poor little opinion as if they were the most ruthless and highly trained lawyers, and on the opposing side.

After Charlie was diagnosed, Lucien had just enough time to understand perfectly what that was to mean. When he was exhausted enough to sleep, he slept as though under heavy anaesthetic during an amputation. The pain was not alleviated, but it had been made inscrutable. A frightful thing seemed to lie on top of him, heavy and cold. All night long he would struggle to throw it off, but when dawn delivered him to consciousness, he understood what it was, and that it would never go away.

During his waking hours, the food on his plate would abruptly lose its taste, the painting he was studying would bleach off the canvas, the friend he was talking to would turn into a stranger. And then, one day, he was living in a world all made out of paper, where the sun was a wad of old newspapers and the only sounds were the sounds of tearing paper.

He spoke with Rose and Isaac frequently during Charlie's illness, and they came to New York for her memorial service, where they sat self-consciously and miserably among Lucien and Charlie's attractive friends. He took them to the airport for their return to the Midwest, embraced them warmly, and as they shuffled toward the departure door with the other passengers, turning once to wave, he breathed a sigh of relief all that, at least, was over, too.

As his senses began to revive, he felt a brief pang — he would miss, in a minor way, the heartrending buffoonery of Charlie's sister and brother-in-law. After all, it had been part of his life with Charlie, even if it had been the only annoying part.

But Charlie's death, instead of setting him utterly, blessedly adrift in his grief, had left him anchored permanently offshore of her family like an island. After a long silence, the infuriating calls started up again. The feudal relationship was apparently inalterable.

---

to solicit to ask for, to request

demurral here: objection

to hazard a guess to make a guess

inscrutable unergründlich

wad a small round bundle

pang strong, sudden pain

buffoonery stupid, annoying behaviour

The terrorist attacks of 9/11
On September 11, 2001, Al-Qaeda terrorists hijacked four passenger aircrafts on the US east coast. Two planes hit the World Trade Center's Twin Towers in New York; one plane was steered into the Pentagon in Washington, DC; one plane crashed into an open field near Shanksville, Pennsylvania. The number of fatal victims was 2,977.

CONTEXT

When they'd moved in, it probably *was* the best view on the planet. Then, one morning, out of a clear blue sky, it became, for a while, probably the worst.

For a long time now they've been able to hang out here on the terrace without anyone running inside to be sick or bursting into tears or diving under something at a loud noise or even just making macabre jokes or wondering what sort of debris is settling into their drinks. These days they rarely see — as for a time they invariably did — the sky igniting, the stinking smoke bursting out of it like lava, the tiny figures raining down from the shattered tower as Lyle faints.

But now it's unclear what they are, in fact, looking at.

INFORMATION

What would Charlie say about the show that's about to go up? It's work by a youngish Belgian painter who arrived, splashily, on the scene sometime after Charlie's departure.

It's good work, but these days Lucien can't get terribly excited about any of the shows. The vibrancy of his brain arranging itself in response to something of someone else's making, the heart's little leap — his gift, reliable for so many years, is gone. Or mostly gone; it's flattened out into something banal and tepid. It's as if he's got some part that's simply worn out and needs replacing. Let's hope it's still available, he thinks.

How *did* he get so old? The usual stupid question. One had snickered all one's life as the plaintive old geezers doddered about baffled, as if looking for a misplaced sock, tugging one's sleeve, asking sheepishly: *How did I get so old?*

The mere sight of one's patiently blank expression turned them vicious. *It will happen to you*, they'd raged.

Well, all right, it would. But not in the ridiculous way it had happened to them. And yet, here he is, he and his friends, falling like so much landfill into the dump of old age. Or at least struggling desperately to balance on the brink. Yet one second ago, running so swiftly toward it, they hadn't even seen it.

And what had happened to his youth? Unlike a misplaced sock, it isn't anywhere; it had dissolved in the making of him. Surprising that after Charlie's death he did not take the irreversible step. He'd had no appetite to live. But the body has its own appetite, apparently — that pitiless need to continue with its living, which has so many disguises and so many rationales.

---

leap jump

tepid indifferent, lukewarm

to snicker (AE) to giggle, to laugh
geezers (pl., infml.) odd person, usually old
baffled confused
*****vicious** extremely unkind; evil-minded, violent

*****dump** *Halde*

*****disguise** *Verkleidung*

A deep embarrassment has been stalking him. Every time he lets his guard down these days, there it is. Because it's become clear: he and even the most dissolute among his friends have glided through their lives on the assumption that the sheer fact of their existence has in some way made the world a better place. As deranged as it sounds now, a better place. Not a leafy bower, maybe, but still, a somewhat better place — more tolerant, more amenable to the wonderful adventures of the human mind and the human body, more capable of outrage against injustice …

dissolute (fml.) *zügellos, ausschweifend*

bower (fml.) pleasant garden area protected by trees

For shame! One has been shocked, all one's life, to learn of the blind eye turned to children covered with bruises and welts, the blind eye turned to the men who came at night for the neighbors. And yet … And yet one has clung to the belief that the sun shining inside one's head is evidence of sunshine elsewhere.

Not everywhere, of course. Obviously, at every moment something terrible is being done to someone somewhere — one can't really know about each instance of it!

Then again, how far away does something have to be before you have the right to not really know about it?

Sometime after Charlie's death, Lucien resumed throwing his parties. He and his friends continued to buy art and make art, to drink and reflect. They voted responsibly, they gave to charity, they read the paper assiduously. And while they were basking in their exclusive sunshine, what had happened to the planet? Lucien gazes at his glass of wine, his eyes stinging.

to resume sth (fml.) to start sth again

HOMESICK

Nathaniel was eight or nine when his aunt and uncle had come out to the Midwest to visit the family, lustrous and clever and comfortable and humorous and affectionate with one another, in their soft, stylish clothing. They'd brought books with them to read. When they talked to each other — and they habitually did — not only did they take turns, but also, what one said followed on what the other said. What world could they have come from? What was the world in which beings like his aunt and uncle could exist?

lustrous shiny

A world utterly unlike his parents', that was for sure — a world of freedom and lightness and beauty and the ardent exchange of ideas and … and … *fun.*

A great longing rose up in Nathaniel like a flower with a lovely, haunting fragrance. When he was ready, he'd thought —

★ **fragrance** *Duft*

when he was able, when he was worthy, he'd get to the world from which his magic aunt and uncle had once briefly appeared.

The evidence, though, kept piling up that he was not worthy. Because even when he finished school, he simply didn't budge. How unfair it was — his friends had flown off so easily, as if going to New York were nothing at all.

Immediately after graduation, Madison found himself a job at a fancy New York PR firm. And it seemed that there was a place out there on the trading floor of the Stock Exchange for Amity. And Lyle had suddenly exhibited an astonishing talent for sound design and engineering, so where else would he sensibly live, either?

Yes, the fact was that only Nathaniel seemed slated to remain behind in their college town. Well, he told himself, his parents were getting on; he would worry, so far away. And he was actually employed as a part-time assistant with an actual architectural firm, whereas in New York the competition, for even the lowliest of such jobs, would be ferocious. And also, he had plenty of time, living where he did, to work on *Passivityman*.

And that's what he told Amity, too, when she'd called one night, four years ago, urging him to take the plunge.

"It's time for you to try, Nathaniel," she said. "It's time to commit. This oddball, slacker stance is getting kind of old, don't you think, kind of stale. You cannot let your life be ruled by fear any longer."

"Fear?" He flinched. "By what fear, exactly, do you happen to believe my life is ruled?"

"Well, I mean, fear of failure, obviously. Fear of mediocrity."

For an instant he thought he might be sick.

"Right," he said. "And why should I fear failure and mediocrity? Failure and mediocrity have such august traditions! Anyhow, what's up with you, Amity?"

She'd been easily distracted, and they chatted on for a while, but when they hung up, he felt very, very strange, as if his apartment had slightly changed shape. Amity was right, he'd thought; it was fear that stood between him and the life he'd meant to be leading.

That was probably the coldest night of the whole, difficult millennium. The timid midwestern sun had basically gone down at the beginning of September; it wouldn't be around much again till May. Black ice glared on the street outside like the cloak of an extra-cruel witch. The sink faucet was dripping into a cracked and stained teacup: *Tick tock tick tock…*

---

to budge to move

slated here: *vorgesehen für etw.*

ferocious fierce, tough

slacker (fml.) sb who is not ambitious and tries to avoid working

* **mediocrity** Mittelmaß

cloak Umhang

What was he *doing*? Once he'd dreamed of designing tranquil and ennobling dwellings, buildings that urged benign relationships, rich inner harmonies; he'd dreamed of meeting fascinating strangers. True, he'd managed to avoid certain pitfalls of middle-class adulthood — he wasn't a white-collar criminal, for example; he wasn't (at least as far as he knew) a total blowhard. But what was he *actually doing*? His most exciting social contact was the radio. He spent his salaried hours in a cinder-block office building, poring over catalogues of plumbing fixtures. The rest of the day — and the whole evening, too — he sat at the little desk his parents had bought for him when he was in junior high, slaving over *Passivityman*, a comic strip that ran in free papers all over parts of the Midwest, a comic strip that was doted on by whole dozens, the fact was, of stoned undergrads.

He was twenty-four years old! Soon he'd be twenty-eight. In a few more minutes he'd be thirty-five, then fifty. Five zero. How had that happened? He was eighty! He could feel his vascular system and brain clogging with paste, he was drooling …

And if history had anything to teach, it was that he'd be broke when he was eighty, too, and that his personal life would still be a disaster.

But wait. Long ago, panic had sent his grandparents and parents scurrying from murderous Europe, with its death camps and pogroms, to the safe harbor of New York. Panic had kept them going as far as the Midwest, where grueling labor enabled them and eventually their children to lead blessedly ordinary lives. And sooner or later, Nathaniel's pounding heart was telling him, that same sure-footed guide, panic, would help him retrace his family's steps all the way back to Manhattan.

OPPORTUNISM

Blip! Charlie scatters again as Lucien's attention wavers from her, and the empty space belonging to her is seized by Miss Mueller.

Huh, but what do you know — death *suits* Miss Mueller! In life she was drab, but now she absolutely throbs with ghoulishness. *You there, Lucien* — the shriek echoes around the gallery — *What are the world's three great religions?*

Zen Buddhism, Jainism, and Sufism, he responds sulkily.

Naughty boy! She cackles flirtatiously. *Bang bang, you're dead!*

THE HALF-LIFE OF PASSIVITY

Passivityman is taking a snooze, his standard response to stress, when the alarm rings. "I'll check it out later, boss," he murmurs.
"You'll check it out *now*, please," his girlfriend and superior, the beautiful Princess Prudence, tells him. "Just put on those grubby corduroys and get out there."
"Aw, is it really *urgent*?" he asks.
"Don't you get it?" she says. "I've been warning you. Episode after episode! And now, from his appliance-rich house on the Moon, Captain Corporation has tightened his Net of Evil around the planet Earth, and he's dragging it out of orbit! The U.S. Congress is selected by pharmaceutical companies, the state of Israel is run by Christian fundamentalists, the folks that haul toxic sludge manufacture cattle feed and process burgers, your sources of news and information are edited by a giant mouse, New York City and Christian fundamentalism are holdings of a family in Kuwait — *and all of it's owned by Captain Corporation!*"
Passivityman rubs his eyes and yawns. "Well gosh, Pru, sure — but, like, what am I supposed to do about it?"
"*I* don't know," Princess Prudence says. "It's hardly my job to figure that out, is it? I mean, *you're* the superhero. Just — just — just go out and do something conspicuously lacking in monetary value! Invent some stinky, profit-proof gloop to pour on stuff. Or, I don't know, whatever. But you'd better do *something*, before it's too late."
"Sounds like it's totally too late already," says Passivityman, reaching for a cigarette.

It was quite a while ago now that Passivityman seemed to throw in the towel. Nathaniel's friends looked at the strip with him and scratched their heads.
"Hm, *I* don't know, Nathaniel," Amity said. "This episode is awfully complicated. I mean, Passivityman's seeming kind of passive-*aggressive*, actually."
"Can Passivityman not be bothered any longer to protect the abject with his greed-repelling Shield of Sloth?" Lyle asked.
"It's not going to be revealed that Passivityman is a double agent, is it?" Madison said. "I mean, what about his undying struggle against corporate-model efficiency?"
"The truth is, I don't really know what's going on with him," Nathaniel said. "I was thinking that maybe, unbeknownst to

himself, he's come under the thrall of his morally neutral, transgendering twin, Ambiguityperson."

"Yeah," Madison said. "But I mean, the problem here is that he's just not dealing with the paradox of his own being — he seems kind of *intellectually* passive …"

Oh, dear. Poor Passivityman. He was a *tired* old crime fighter. Nathaniel sighed; it was hard to live the way his superhero lived — constantly vigilant against the premature conclusion, scrupulously rejecting the vulgar ambition, rigorously deferring judgment and action … and all for the greater good.

"Huh, well, I guess he's sort of losing his superpowers," Nathaniel said.

The others looked away uncomfortably.

"Oh, it's probably just one of those slumps," Amity said. "I'm sure he'll be back to normal, soon."

But by now, Nathaniel realizes, he's all but stopped trying to work on *Passivityman*.

thrall (fml.) control, influence

vigilant wachsam
to defer sth etw. aufschieben, verschieben

⬆ Who is Passivityman?

ALL THIS

Thanks for pointing that out, Miss Mueller. Yes, humanity seems to have reverted by a millennium or so. Goon squads, purporting to represent each of the *world's three great religions* — as they used to be called to fifth-graders, and perhaps still so misleadingly are — have deployed themselves all over the map, apparently in hopes of annihilating not only each other, but absolutely everyone, themselves excepted.

Just a few weeks earlier, Lucien was on a plane heading home from Los Angeles, and over the loudspeaker, the pilot requested that all Christians on board raise their hands. The next sickening instants provided more than enough time for conjecture as to who, exactly, was about to be killed — Christians or non-Christians. And then the pilot went on to ask those who had raised their hands to talk about their "faith" with the others.

Well, better him than Rose and Isaac; that would have been two sure heart attacks, right there. And anyhow, why should he be so snooty about religious fanaticism? Stalin managed to kill off over thirty million people in the name of no god at all, and not so very long ago.

At the moment when *all this* — as Lucien thinks of it — began, the moment when a few ordinary-looking men carrying box cutters sped past the limits of international negotiation and

goon squad Schlägertrupp

to annihilate to extinguish, to kill

conjecture (fml.) guess, assumption

the frontiers of technology, turning his miraculous city into a nightmare and hurling the future into a void, Lucien was having his croissant and coffee.

The television was saying something. Lucien wheeled around and stared at it, then turned to look out the window; downtown, black smoke was already beginning to pollute the perfect, silken September morning. On the screen, the ruptured, flaming colossus was shedding veils of tiny black specks.

All circuits were busy, of course; the phone might as well have been a toy. Lucien was trembling as he shut the door of the apartment behind him. His face was wet. Outside, he saw that the sky in the north was still insanely blue.

THE AGE OF DROSS

Well, superpowers are probably a feature of youth, like Wendy's ability to fly around with that creepy Peter Pan. Or maybe they belonged to a loftier period of history. It seems that Captain Corporation, his swaggering lieutenants and massed armies have actually neutralized Passivityman's superpower. Passivityman's astonishing reserves of resistance have vanished in the quicksand of Captain Corporation's invisible account books. His rallying cry, No way, which once rang out over the land, demobilizing millions, has been altered by Captain Corporation's co-optophone into, Whatever. And the superpowers of Nathaniel's friends have been seriously challenged, too. Challenged, or … outgrown.

Amity's superpower, her gift for exploiting systemic weaknesses, had taken a terrible beating several years ago when the gold she spun out on the trading floor turned — just like everyone else's — into straw. And subsequently, she plummeted from job to job, through layers of prestige, ending up behind a counter in a fancy department store where she sold overpriced skin-care products.

Now, of course, the sale of *Inner Beauty Secrets* — her humorous, lightly fictionalized account of her experiences there with her clients — indicates that perhaps her powers are regenerating. But time will tell.

Madison's superpower, an obtuse, patrician equanimity in the face of damning fact, was violently and irremediably terminated one day when a girl arrived at the door asking for him. "I'm your sister," she told him. "Sorry," Madison said, "I've never seen you before in my life." "Hang on," the girl said. "I'm just getting to that."

For months afterward, Madison kept everyone awake late into

the night repudiating all his former beliefs, his beautiful blue eyes whirling around and his hair standing on end as if he'd stuck his hand into a socket. He quit his lucrative PR job and denounced the firm's practices in open letters to media watchdog groups (copies to his former boss). The many women who'd been running after him did a fast about-face.

Amity called him a "bitter skeptic"; he called Amity a "dupe." The heated quarrel that followed has tapered off into an uneasy truce, at best.

Lyle's superpower back in school was his spectacular level of aggrievedness and his ability to get anyone at all to feel sorry for him. But later, doing sound with a Paris-based dance group, Lyle met Jahan, who was doing the troupe's lighting.

Jahan is (a) as handsome as a prince, (b) as charming, as intelligent, as noble in his thoughts, feelings, and actions as a prince, and (c) a prince, at least of some attenuated sort. So no one feels sorry for Lyle at all any longer, and Lyle has apparently left the pleasures of even *self*-pity behind him without a second thought.

A while ago, though, Jahan was mistakenly arrested in some sort of sweep near Times Square, and when he was finally released from custody, he moved to London, and Lyle does nothing but pine, when he can't be in London himself.

"Well, look on the bright side," Nathaniel said. "At least you might get your superpower back."

"You know Nathaniel ..." Lyle said. He looked at Nathaniel for a moment, and then an unfamiliar kindness modified his expression. He patted Nathaniel on the shoulder and went on his way.

Yikes. So much for Lyle's superpower, obviously.

...

"It's great that you got to live here for so long, though," Russell is saying.

Nathaniel has the sudden sensation of his whole four years in New York twisting themselves into an arrow speeding through the air and twanging into the dead center of this evening. All so hard to believe. "This is not happening," he says.

"I think it might really *be* happening, though," Lyle says.

"Fifty percent of respondents say that the event taking place is not occurring," Madison says. "The other fifty percent remain undecided. Clearly, the truth lies somewhere in between."

Soon it might be as if he and Lyle and Madison and Amity had never even lived here. Because this moment is joined to all the other moments they've spent together here, and all of those moments are Right Now. But soon this moment and all the

about-face Kehrtwende
dupe here: naïve person

truce state of peace or agreement

attenuated here: weak, powerless

to pine to wish strongly for sth you cannot have

yikes (infml.) gosh, for God's sake

others will be cut off — in the past, not part of Right Now at all. Yeah, he and his three friends might all be going their separate ways, come to think of it, once they move out.

CONTINUITY

While the sirens screamed, Lucien had walked against the tide of dazed, smoke-smeared people, down into the fuming cauldron, and when he finally reached the police cordon, his feet aching, he wandered along it for hours, searching for Charlie's nephew, among all the other people who were searching for family, friends, lovers.

Oh, that day! One kept waiting — as if a morning would arrive from before that day to take them all along a different track. One kept waiting for that shattering day to unhappen, so that the real — the intended — future, the one that had been implied by the past, could unfold. Hour after hour, month after month, waiting for that day to not have happened.

But it had happened. And now it was always going to have happened. Most likely on the very mornings that first Rose and then Isaac had disembarked at Ellis Island, each clutching some remnant of the world they were never to see again, Lucien was being wheeled in his pram through the genteel world, a few miles uptown, of brownstones.

The city, more than his body, contained his life. His life! The schools he had gone to as a child, the market where his mother had bought the groceries, the park where he had played with his classmates, the restaurants where he had courted Charlie, the various apartments they'd lived in, the apartments of their friends, the gallery, the newsstand on the corner, the dry cleaner's ... The things he did in the course of the day, year after year, the people he encountered.

...

A sticky layer of crematorium ash settled over the whole of Matsumoto's neighborhood, even inside, behind closed windows, as thick in places as turf, and water was unavailable for a time. Nathaniel and his friends all stayed elsewhere, of course, for a few weeks. When it became possible, Lucien sent crews down to Matsumoto's loft to scour the place and restore the art.

FAREWELL

A memorandum hangs in Mr. Matsumoto's lobby, that appeared several months ago when freakish blackouts were rolling over the city.
Emergency Tips from the Management urges residents to assemble a Go Bag, in the event of an evacuation, as well as an In-Home Survival Kit. Among items to include: a large amount of cash in small denominations, water and nonperishable foods such as granola bars, a wind-up radio, warm clothing and sturdy walking shoes, unscented bleach and an eyedropper for purifying water, plastic sheeting and duct tape, a whistle, a box cutter.
Also recommended is a Household Disaster Plan and the practicing of emergency drills.
A hand-lettered sign next to the elevator says THINK TWICE.

Twenty-eight years old, no superhero, a job that just *might* lead down to a career in underground architecture, a vanishing apartment, a menacing elevator ... Maybe he should view Mr. Matsumoto's return as an opportunity, and regroup. Maybe he should *do* something — take matters in hand. Maybe he should go try to find Delphine, for example.
But how? He hasn't heard from her, and she could be anywhere now; she'd mentioned Bucharest, she'd mentioned Havana, she'd mentioned Shanghai, she'd mentioned Istanbul ...
He'd met her at one of his uncle's parties. There was the usual huge roomful of people wearing strangely pleated black clothes, like the garments of a somber devotional sect, and there she was in electric-blue taffeta, amazingly tall and narrow, lazy and nervous, like an electric bluebell.
She favored men nearly twice Nathaniel's age and millions of times richer, but for a while she let Nathaniel come over to her apartment and play her his favorite CDs. They drank perfumey infusions from chipped porcelain cups, or vodka. Delphine could become thrillingly drunk, and she smoked, letting long columns of ash form on her tarry, unfiltered cigarettes.
One night, when he lost his keys, she let him come over and sleep in her bed while she went out, and when the sky fell, she actually let him sleep on her floor for a week.
Her apartment was filled with puffy, silky little sofas, and old, damaged mirrors and tarnished candlesticks, and tall vases filled with slightly wilting flowers. It smelled like powder and tea and cigarettes and her Abyssinian cats, which prowled the

bleach here: *Bleichmittel*
duct tape (AE) *Klebeband*

tarry containing much tar (e. g. in cigarettes) and therefore very strong

candlestick object for holding a candle

rug Teppich

savannas of the white, long-haired rugs or posed on the marble mantelpiece.

Delphine's father was Armenian and he lived in Paris, which according to Delphine was a bore. Her mother was Chilean. Delphine's English had been acquired at a boarding school in Kent for dull-witted rich girls and castaways, like herself, from everywhere.

castaway survivor in shipwreck

She spoke many languages, she was self-possessed and beautiful and fascinating. She could have gone to live anywhere. And she had come, like Nathaniel, to New York.

"But look at it now," she'd raged. Washington was dropping bombs on Afghanistan and then Iraq, and every few weeks there was a flurry of alerts in kindergarten colors indicating the likelihood of terrorist attacks: yellow, orange, red, *duck!*

"Do you know how I get the news here?" Delphine said. "From your newspapers? Please! From your newspapers I learn what restaurant has opened. News I learn in taxis, from the drivers. And how do they get it? From their friends and relatives back home, in Pakistan or Uzbekistan or Somalia. The drivers sit around at the airport, swapping information, and they can tell you *anything*. But do you ask? Or sometimes I talk to my friends in Europe. Do you know what they're saying about you over there?"

"Please don't say 'you,' Delphine," he had said faintly.

to stifle to suppress

"Oh, yes, here it's not like stuffy old Europe, where everything is stifled by tradition and trauma. Here you're able to speak freely, within reason, of course, and isn't it wonderful that you all happen to want to say exactly what they want you to say? Do you know how many people you're killing over there? No, how would you? Good, just keep your eyes closed, panic, don't ask any questions, and you can speak freely about whatever you like. And if you have any suspicious-looking neighbors, be sure to tell the police. You had everything here, everything, and you threw it all away in one second."

She was so beautiful; he'd gazed at her as if he were already remembering her. "Please don't say 'you,'" he murmured again.

"Poor Nathaniel," she said. "This place is nothing now but a small-minded, mean-spirited provincial town."

THE AGE OF DIGITAL REASONING

One/two. On/off. The plane crashes/doesn't crash.
The plane he took from L.A. didn't crash. It wasn't used as a missile to blow anything up, and not even one passenger was

shot or stabbed. Nothing happened. So, what's the problem? What's the difference between having been on that flight and having been on any other flight in his life?

Oh, what's the point of thinking about death all the time! Think about it or not, you die. Besides — and here's something that sure hasn't changed — you don't have to do it more than once. And as you don't have to do it *less* than once, either, you might as well do it on the plane. Maybe there's no special problem these days. Maybe the problem is just that he's old. Or maybe his nephew's is the last generation that will remember what it had once felt like to blithely assume there would be a future — at least a future like the one that had been implied by the past they'd all been familiar with.

But the future actually ahead of them, it's now obvious, had itself been implied by a past; and the terrible day that pointed them toward that future had been prepared for a long, long time, though it had been prepared behind a curtain.

It was as if there had been a curtain, a curtain painted with the map of the earth, its oceans and continents, with Lucien's delightful city. The planes struck, tearing through the curtain of that blue September morning, exposing the dark world that lay right behind it, of populations ruthlessly exploited, inflamed with hatred, and tired of waiting for change to happen by.

The stump of the ruined tower continued to smolder far into the fall, and an unseasonable heat persisted. When the smoke lifted, all kinds of other events, which had been prepared behind a curtain, too, were revealed. Flags waved in the brisk air of fear, files were demanded from libraries and hospitals, droning helicopters hung over the city, and heavily armed policemen patrolled the parks. Meanwhile, one read that executives had pocketed the savings of their investors and the pensions of their employees.

The wars in the East were hidden behind a thicket of language: *patriotism, democracy, loyalty, freedom* — the words bounced around, changing purpose, as if they were made out of some funny plastic. What did they actually refer to? It seemed that they all might refer to money.

Were the sudden power outages and spiking level of unemployment related? And what was causing them? The newspapers seemed for the most part to agree that the cause of both

power outage *Stromausfall*

was terrorism. But lots of people said they were both the consequence of corporate theft. It was certainly all beyond Lucien! Things that had formerly appeared to be distinct, or even at odds, now seemed to have been smoothly blended, to mutual advantage. Provocation and retribution, arms manufacture and statehood, oil and war, commerce and dogma, and the spinning planet seemed to be boiling them all together at the center of the earth into a poison syrup. Enemies had soared toward each other from out of the past to unite in a joyous fireball; planes had sheared through the heavy, painted curtain and from the severed towers an inexhaustible geyser had erupted.

...

Styles of pets revolved rapidly, as if the city's residents were searching for a type of animal that would express a stance appropriate to the horrifying assault, which for all anyone knew was only the first of many.

For a couple of months everyone was walking cute, perky things. Then Lucien saw snarling hounds everywhere and the occasional boa constrictor draped around its owner's shoulders. After that, it was tiny, trembling dogs that traveled in purses and pockets.

New York had once been the threshold of an impregnable haven, then the city had become in an instant the country's open wound, and now it was the occasion — the pretext! — for killing and theft and legislative horrors all over the world. The air stank from particulate matter — chemicals and asbestos and blood and scorched bone. People developed coughs and strange rashes.

What should be done, and to whom? Almost any word, even between friends, could ignite a sheet of flame. What were the bombings for? First one imperative was cited and then another; the rationales shifted hastily to cover successive gaps in credibility. Bills were passed containing buried provisions, and loopholes were triumphantly discovered — alarming elasticities or rigidities in this law or that. One was sick of trying to get a solid handle on the stream of pronouncements — it was like endlessly trying to sort little bits of paper into stacks when a powerful fan was on.

Friends in Europe and Asia sent him clippings about his own country. *What's all this,* they asked — secret arrests and detentions, his president capering about in military uniform, crazy talk of preemptive nuclear strikes? Why were they releasing a big science fiction horror movie over there, about the emperor of everything everywhere, for which the whole world was required to buy tickets? What on earth was going on with them all, why were they all so silent? Why did they all seem so confused?

How was he to know, Lucien thought. If his foreign friends had such great newspapers, why didn't *they* tell *him*!

No more smiles from strangers on the street! Well, it was reasonable to be frightened; everyone had seen what those few men were able do with the odds and ends in their pockets. The heat lifted, and then there was unremitting cold. No one lingered to joke and converse in the course of their errands, but instead hurried irritably along, like people with bad consciences.

And always in front of you now was the sight that had been hidden by the curtain, of all those irrepressibly, murderously angry people.

Private life shrank to nothing. All one's feelings had been absorbed by an arid wasteland — policy, strategy, goals. One's past, one's future, one's ordinary daily pleasures were like dusty little curios on a shelf.

Lucien continued defiantly throwing his parties, but as the murky wars dragged on, he stopped. It was impossible to have fun or to want to have fun. It was one thing to have fun if the sun was shining generally, quite another thing to have fun if it was raining blood everywhere but on your party. What did he and his friends really have in common, anyway? Maybe nothing more than their level of privilege.

In restaurants and cafés all over the city, people seemed to have changed. The good-hearted, casually wasteful festival was over. In some places the diners were sullen and dogged, as if they felt accused of getting away with something.

In other places, the gaiety was cranked up to the level of completely unconvincing hysteria. For a long miserable while, in fact, the city looked like a school play about war profiteering. The bars were overflowing with very young people from heaven only knew where, in hideous, ludicrously showy clothing, spending massive amounts of money on green, pink, and orange cocktails, and laughing at the top of their lungs, as if at filthy jokes.

No, not like a school play — like a movie, though the performances and the direction were crude. The loud, ostensibly carefree young people appeared to be extras recruited from the suburbs, and yet sometime in the distant future, people

errand here: short trip to do some business

curio object, thing; curiosity

diner here: sb eating in a restaurant
sullen in a gloomy, silent mood
dogged verbissen
gaiety feeling of fun

hideous ugly, scary

seeing such a movie might think oh, yes, that was a New York that existed once, say, at the end of the millennium.

It was Lucien's city, Lucien's times, and yet what he appeared to be living in wasn't the actual present — it was an inaccurate representation of the *past*. True, it looked something like the New York that existed before *all this* began, but Lucien remembered, and he could see: the costumes were not quite right, the hairstyles were not quite right, the gestures and the dialogue were not quite right.

Oh. Yes. Of course none of it was quite right — the movie was a *propaganda* movie. And now it seems that the propaganda movie has done its job: things, in a grotesque sense, are back to normal.

Money is flowing a bit again, most of the flags have folded up, those nervewracking terror alerts have all but stopped, the kids in the restaurants have calmed down, no more rolling blackouts, and the dogs on the street encode no particular messages. Once again, people are concerned with getting on with their lives. Once again, the curtain has dropped.

Except that people seem a little bit nervous, a little uncomfortable, a little wary. Because you can't help sort of knowing that what you're seeing is only the curtain. And you can't help guessing what might be going on behind it.

THE FURTHER IN THE PAST THINGS ARE, THE BIGGER THEY BECOME

Nathaniel remembers more and more rather than less and less vividly the visit of his uncle and aunt to the Midwest during his childhood.

He'd thought his aunt Charlie was the most beautiful woman he'd ever seen. And for all he knows, she really was. He never saw her after that one visit; by the time he came to New York and reconnected with Uncle Lucien she had been dead for a long time. She would still have been under fifty when she died — crushed, his mother had once, in a mood, implied, by the weight of her own pretensions.

His poor mother! She had cooked, cleaned, and fretted for ... months, it had seemed, in preparation for that visit of Uncle Lucien and Aunt Charlie. And observing in his memory the four grown-ups, Nathaniel can see an awful lot of white knuckles.

wary cautious

pretension belief that you can succeed or that you are important

knuckle Knöchel

He remembers his mother picking up a book Aunt Charlie had left lying on the kitchen table, glancing at it and putting it back down with a tiny shrug and a lifted eyebrow. "You don't approve?" Aunt Charlie said, and Nathaniel is shocked to see, in his memory, that she is tense.

His mother, having gained the advantage, makes another bitter little shrug. "I'm sure it's over my head," she says.

When the term of the visit came to an end, they dropped Uncle Lucien and Aunt Charlie at the airport. His brother was driving, too fast. Nathaniel can hear himself announcing in his child's piercing voice, *"I want to live in New York like Uncle Lucien and Aunt Charlie!"* His exile's heart was brimming, but it was clear from his mother's profile that she was braced for an execution.

"Slow *down*, Bernie!" his mother said, but Bernie hadn't. "Big shot," she muttered, though it was unclear at whom this was directed — whether at his brother or himself or his father, or his Uncle Lucien, or at Aunt Charlie herself.

BACK TO NORMAL

Do dogs have to fight sadness as tirelessly as humans do? They seem less involved with retrospect, less involved in dread and anticipation. Animals other than humans appear to be having a more profound experience of the present. But who's to say? Clearly their feelings are intense, and maybe grief and anxiety darken all their days. Maybe that's why they've acquired their stripes and polka dots and fluffiness — to cheer themselves up.

Poor old Earth, an old sponge, a honeycomb of empty mine shafts and dried wells. While he and his friends were wittering on, the planet underfoot had been looted. The waterways glint with weapons-grade plutonium, sneaked on barges between one wrathful nation and another, the polar ice caps melt, Venice sinks.

In the horrible old days in Europe when Rose and Isaac were hunted children, it must have been pretty clear to them how to behave, minute by minute. Men in jackboots? Up to the attic! But even during that time when it was so dangerous to speak out, to act courageously, heroes emerged. Most of them died fruitlessly, of course, and unheralded. But now there are even monuments to some of them, and information about such people is always coming to light.

Maybe there really is no problem, maybe everything really is

to brace for sth to get ready for sth

honeycomb *Bienenstock*

* **to loot sth** *etw. plündern*
barge cargo ship

back to normal and maybe the whole period will sink peacefully away, to be remembered only by scholars. But if it should end, instead, in dire catastrophe, whom will the monuments of the future commemorate?

Today, all day long, Lucien has seen the president's vacant, stricken expression staring from the ubiquitous television screens. He seemed to be talking about positioning weapons in space, colonizing the moon.

Open your books to page 167, class, Miss Mueller shrieks. *What do you see?*
Lucien sighs.
The pages are thin and sort of shiny. The illustrations are mostly black and white.
This one's a photograph of a statue, an emperor, apparently, wearing his stone toga and his stone wreath. The real people, the living people, mill about just beyond the picture's confines, but Lucien knows more or less what they look like — he's seen illustrations of them, too. He knows what a viaduct is and that the ancient Romans went to plays and banquets and that they had a code of law from which his country's own is derived. Are the people hidden by the picture frightened? Do they hear the stones working themselves loose, the temples and houses and courts beginning to crumble?
Out the window, the sun is just a tiny, tiny bit higher today than it was at this exact instant yesterday. After school, he and Robbie Stern will go play soccer in the park. In another month it will be bright and warm.

PARADISE

So, Mr. Matsumoto will be coming back, and things seem pretty much as they did when he left. The apartment is clean, the cats are healthy, the art is undamaged, and the view from the terrace is exactly the same, except there's that weird, blank spot where the towers used to stand.
"Open the next?" Madison says, holding up a bottle of champagne. "Strongly agree, agree, undecided, disagree, strongly disagree."
"Strongly agree," Lyle says.
"Thanks," Amity says.
"Okay," Russell says. "I'm in."
Nathaniel shrugs and holds out his glass.
Madison pours. "Polls indicate that 100 percent of the American public approves heavy drinking," he says.

"Oh, god, Madison," Amity says. "Can't we ever just *drop* it? Can't we ever just have a nice time?"

Madison looks at her for a long moment. "Drop what?" he says, evenly.

But no one wants to get into *that*.

When Nathaniel was in his last year at college, his father began to suffer from heart trouble. It was easy enough for Nathaniel to come home on the weekends, and he'd sit with his father, gazing out the window as the autumnal light gilded the dry grass and the fallen leaves glowed.

His father talked about his own time at school, working night and day, the pride his parents had taken in him, the first college student in their family.

Over the years Nathaniel's mother and father had grown gentler with one another and with him. Sometimes after dinner and the dishes, they'd all go out for a treat. Nathaniel would wait, an acid pity weakening his bones, while his parents debated worriedly over their choices, as if nobody ever had before or would ever have again the opportunity to eat ice cream.

treat sth special

Just last night, he dreamed about Delphine, a delicious champagne-style dream, full of love and beauty — a weird, high-quality love, a feeling he doesn't remember ever having had in his waking life — a pure, wholehearted, shining love.

It hangs around him still, floating through the air out on the terrace — fragrant, shimmering, fading.

WAITING

The bell is about to ring. Closing his book Lucien hears the thrilling crash as the bloated empire tumbles down.

Gold star, Lucien! Miss Mueller cackles deafeningly, and then she's gone.

Charlie's leaving, too. Lucien lifts his glass; she glances back across the thin, inflexible divide.

From farther than the moon she sees the children of some distant planet study pictures in their text: there's Rose and Isaac at their kitchen table, Nathaniel out on Mr. Matsumoto's terrace, Lucien alone in the dim gallery — and then the children turn the page.

The Scribner Anthology of Contemporary Short Fiction: 50 North America Short Stories since 1970. Eds. Lex Williford, Michael Martone. 2nd ed. New York: Touchstone, 2007, pp. 190–213.

Charity
Charles Baxter

1

He had fallen into bad trouble. He had worked in Ethiopia for a year – teaching in a school and lending a hand at a medical clinic. He had eaten all the local foods and been stung by the many airborne insects. When he'd returned to the States, he'd brought back an infection — the inflammation in his knees and his back and his shoulders was so bad that sometimes he could hardly stand up. Probably a viral arthritis, his doctor said. It happens. Here: have some painkillers.

Borrowing a car, he drove down from Minneapolis to the Mayo Clinic, where after two days of tests the doctors informed him that they would have no firm diagnosis for the next month or so. Back in Minneapolis, through a friend of a friend, he visited a wildcat homeopathy treatment center known for traumatic-pain-relief treatments. The center, in a strip mall storefront claiming to be a weight loss clinic (WEIGHT NO MORE), gave him megadoses of meadowsweet, a compound chemically related to aspirin. After two months without health insurance or prescription coverage, he had emptied his bank account, and he gazed at the future with shy dread.

Through another friend of a friend, he managed to get his hands on a few superb prescription painkillers, the big ones, gifts from heaven. With the aid of these pills, he felt like himself again. He blessed his own life. He cooked some decent meals; he called his boyfriend in Seattle; he went around town looking for a job; he made plans to get himself to the Pacific Northwest. When the drugs ran out and the pain returned, worse this time, like being stabbed in his elbows and shoulders, along with the novelty of addiction's chills and fevers, the friend of a friend told him that if he wanted more pills at the going street rate, he had better go see Black Bird. He could find Black Bird at the bar of a club, the Inner Circle, on Hennepin Avenue. "He's always there," the friend of a friend said. "He's there now. He reads. The guy sits there studying Shakespeare. Used to be a scholar or something. Pretends to be a Native American, one of those imposter types. Very easy to spot. I'll tell him you're coming."

The next Wednesday, he found Black Bird at the end of the Inner Circle bar near the broken jukebox and the sign for the men's room. The club's walls had been built from limestone and rust-red brick and sported no decorative motifs of any kind. If you needed decorations around you when you drank, you went somewhere else. The peculiar orange lighting was so dim that Quinn couldn't figure out how Black Bird could read at all.

Quinn approached him gingerly. Black Bird's hair went down to his shoulders. The gray in it looked as if it had been applied with chalk. He wore bifocals and moved his finger down the page as he read. Nearby was a half-consumed bottle of 7 Up.

"Excuse me. Are you Black Bird?"

Without looking up, the man said, "Why do you ask?"

"I'm Quinn." He held out his hand. Black Bird did not take it. "My friend Morrow told me about you."

"Ah huh," Black Bird said. He glanced up with an impatient expression before returning to his book. Quinn examined the text. Black Bird was reading *Othello*, the third act.

"Morrow said I should come see you. There's something I need."

Black Bird said nothing.

"I need it pretty bad," Quinn said, his hand trembling inside his pocket. He wasn't used to talking to people like this. When Black Bird didn't respond, Quinn said, "You're reading *Othello*." Quinn had acquired a liberal arts degree from a college in Iowa, where he had majored in global political solutions, and he felt that he had to assert himself. "The handkerchief. And Iago, right?"

Black Bird nodded. "This isn't *College Bowl*," he said dismissively. With his finger stopped on the page, he said, "What do you want from me?"

Quinn whispered the name of the drug that made him feel human.

"What a surprise," said Black Bird. "Well, well. How do I know that you're not a cop? You a cop, Mr. Quinn?"

"No."

"Because I don't know what you're asking me or what you're talking about. I'm a peaceful man sitting here reading this book and drinking this 7 Up."

"Yes," Quinn said.

"You could always come back in four days," Black Bird said. "You could always bring some money." He mentioned a price for a certain number of painkillers. "I have to get the ducks in a row."

"That's a lot of cash," Quinn said. Then, after thinking it over, he said, "All right." He did not feel that he had many options these days.

---

to sport here: to display, to show

bifocals eyeglasses with two distinct sections, one for seeing near and one for seeing further away

★ **to acquire a degree** to graduate from college or university
★ **liberal arts** *Geisteswissenschaften*
★ **to major in sth** *etw. als Hauptfach studieren*
to assert oneself *sich behaupten*
dismissively showing contempt

to get the ducks in a row to get your life organized

Black Bird looked up at him with an expression devoid of interest or curiosity.

"Do you read, Mr. Quinn?" he asked. "Everybody should read something. Otherwise we all fall down into the pit of ignorance. Many are down there. Some people fall in it forever. Their lives mean nothing. They should not exist." Black Bird spoke these words in a bland monotone.

"I don't know what to read," Quinn told him, his legs shaking.

"Too bad," Black Bird said. "Next time you come here, bring a book. I need proof you exist. The Minneapolis Public Library is two blocks away. But if you come back, bring the money. Otherwise, there's no show."

Quinn was living very temporarily in a friend's basement in Northeast Minneapolis. His parents, in a traditional Old World gesture, had disowned him after he had come out, so he couldn't call on them for support. They had uttered several unforgettable verdicts about his character, sworn they would never see him again, and that was that.

He had a sister who lived in Des Moines with her husband and two children. She did not like what she called Quinn's "sexual preferences" and had a tendency to hang up on him. None of his friends from high school had any money he could borrow; the acquaintance in whose basement he was staying was behind on his rent. His student debt had been taken up by a collection agency, which was calling him three times a day. Quinn's boyfriend in Seattle, a field rep for a medical supply company, had a thing about people borrowing money. He might break up with Quinn if Quinn asked him for a loan. He could be prickly, the boyfriend, and the two of them were still on a trial basis anyway. They had met in Africa and had fallen in love over there. The love might not travel if Quinn brought up the subject of debts or his viral arthritis and inflammation or the drug habit he had recently acquired.

Now that the painkillers had run out, a kind of groggy unfocused physical discomfort had become Quinn's companion day and night. He lived in the house that the pain had designed for him. The Mayo Clinic had not called him back, and the meadowsweet's effect was like a cup of water dropped on a house fire. Sometimes the pain started in Quinn's knees and circled around Quinn's back until it located itself in his shoulders, like exploratory surgery performed using a Swiss Army knife. He had acquired the jitters and a runny nose and a swollen tongue and cramps. He couldn't sleep and had diarrhea. He was a mess, and the knowledge of the mess he had become made the mess worse. The necessity of opiates became a supreme idea that forced out all the other ideas until only one thought occupied Quinn's mind: *Get those painkillers*. He didn't think he was a goner yet, though.

He could no longer tell his dreams from his waking life. The things around him began to take on the appearance of stage props made from cardboard. Other people — pedestrians — looked like shadow creatures giving off a stinky perfume.

In the basement room where he slept, there was, leaning against the wall, a baseball bat, a Louisville Slugger, and one night after dark, in a dreamlike hallucinatory fever, he took it across the Hennepin Avenue Bridge to a park along the Mississippi, where he hid hotly shivering behind a tree until the right sort of prosperous person walked by. Quinn felt as if he were under orders to do what he was about to do. The man he chose wore a T-shirt and jeans and seemed fit but not so strong as to be dangerous, and after rushing out from the shadows, Quinn hit him with the baseball bat in the back of his legs. He had aimed for the back of the legs so he wouldn't shatter the guy's kneecaps. When Quinn's victim fell down, Quinn reached into the man's trouser pocket and pulled out his wallet and ran away with it, dropping the Slugger into the river as he crossed the bridge.

Back in his friend's basement, Quinn examined the wallet's contents. His hands were trembling again, and he couldn't see properly, and he wasn't sure he was awake, but he could make out that the name on the driver's license was Benjamin Takemitsu. The man didn't look Japanese in the driver's license photo, but Quinn didn't think much about it until he'd finished counting the cash, which amounted to $321, an adequate sum for a few days' relief. At that point he gazed more closely at the photo and saw that Takemitsu appeared to be intelligently thoughtful. What had he done to this man? Familiar pain flared behind Quinn's knees and in his neck, punishment he recognized that he deserved, and the pain pushed out everything else.

He called his boyfriend in Seattle. In a panic he told him that he had robbed someone named Benny Takemitsu, that he had used a baseball bat. The boyfriend said. "You've had a bad dream, Matty. That didn't happen. You would never do such a thing. Go back to sleep, sweetheart, and I'll call you tomorrow."

After that he lay awake wondering what had become of the person he had once been, the one who had gone to Africa. To the ceiling he said, "I am no longer myself." He did not know

goner sb who is about to die

* **relief** *Linderung; Erleichterung*

who this new person was, the man whom he had become, but when he finally fell asleep, he saw in his dream one of those shabby castoffs with whom you wouldn't want to have any encounters, any business at all, someone who belonged on the sidewalk with a cardboard sign that read HELP ME. The man was crouched behind a tree in the dark, peering out with feverish eyes. His own face was the face of the castoff.
Somehow he would have to make it up to Benny Takemitsu.

In the Inner Circle, when Quinn entered, Black Bird did not look up. He was seated in his usual place, and once again his finger was traveling down the page. *Cymbeline*, this time, a play that Quinn had never read.
"It's you," Black Bird said.
"Yes," Quinn said.
"Did you bring a book of your own?"
"No."
"All right," Black Bird said. "I can't say I'm surprised."
He then issued elaborate instructions to Quinn about where in the men's room to put the money, and when he, Black Bird, would retrieve it. The entire exchange took over half an hour, though the procedure hardly seemed secret or designed to fool anyone. When Quinn finally returned to his basement room, he had already gulped down two of the pills, and his relief soon grew to a great size. He felt his humanity restored until his mottled face appeared before him in the bathroom mirror, and then he realized belatedly what terrible trouble he was in.
Two days later he disappeared.

2

That was as far as I got whenever I tried to compose an account of what happened to Matty Quinn — my boyfriend, my soulmate, my future life — the man who mistakenly thought I was a tightwad. I *was* very thrifty in Ethiopia, convinced that Americans should not spend large sums in front of people who owned next to nothing. But to Matty I would have given anything. Upon his return to Minneapolis he had called me up and texted and e-mailed me with these small clues about the medical ordeal he was going through, and I had not understood; then he had called to say that he had robbed this Takemitsu, and I had not believed him. Then he disappeared from the world, from his existence and mine.
Two weeks later the investigating officer in the Minneapolis

Police Department (whom I had contacted in my desperation) told me that I could certainly come to survey the city if I wished to. After all, this Officer Erickson said, nothing is stopping you from trying to find your friend, although I understand that your permanent home is in Seattle and you do not know anyone here. It's a free country, so you're welcome to try. However, circumstances being what they are, I wouldn't get your hopes up if I were you. The odds are against it. People go missing, he said. Addicts especially. The street absorbs them. Your friend might be living in a ditch.

He did not say these words with the distancing sarcasm or condescension that straight men sometimes use on queers. He simply sounded bored and hopeless.

Matthew Quinn. First he was Matt. Then he was Matty. These two syllables formed on my tongue as I spoke his name repeatedly into his ear and then into his mouth. That was before he was gone.

This is how we'd met: I had come by the clinic, the one where he worked, to deliver some medical supplies from the company I was then working for, and I saw him near a window whose slatted light fell across the face of a feverish young woman who lay on a bed under mosquito netting. She was resting quietly with her eyes closed and her hand rising to her forehead in an almost unconscious gesture. She was very thin. You could see it in her skinny veined forearms and her prominent cheekbones. On one cheek bone was a J-shaped scar.

Close by, a boy about nine years old sat on a chair, watching her. I had the impression that they had both been there, mother and son, for a week or so. Four other patients immobilized by illness were in other beds scattered around the room. Outside a dog barked in the local language, Amharic, and the air inside remained motionless except for some random agitation under a rattling ceiling fan. The hour was just past midday, and very hot.

That's when I noticed Quinn: he was approaching the woman with a cup in his hand, and after getting himself underneath the mosquito netting, he supported her head as he helped her drink the water, or medicine (I couldn't see what it was), in the cup. Then he turned and, still under the mosquito netting, spoke to the boy in Amharic. His Amharic was better than mine, but I could understand it. He was saying that the boy's mother would be all right but that her recovery would take some time.

The boy nodded.

It was a small, simple gesture of kindness, his remembering to

★ **odds** chances, probability

ditch *Straßengraben*

condescension expression of superiority
★ **queer** homosexual person (noun); homosexual (adj.)

slatted here: dimmed

★ **random** *beliebig, zufällig*

speak to that child. Not everybody would go to the effort. Even when the woman's husband arrived — sweaty, gesticulating, his eyes narrowed with irritation and fear — to complain about the conditions, Quinn smiled, sat him down, and calmed him. Soon the three of them were speaking softly, so that I could not hear what they said.

Young white Americans come to Africa all the time, some to make money, as I did, others in the grip of mostly harmless youthful idealistic delusions. Much of the time, they are operating out of the purest postcolonial sentimentality. I was there on business, for which I don't apologize. But when I saw that this man, Matty Quinn, was indeed doing good works without any hope of reward, it touched me. Compassion was an unthinking habit with him. He was kind by nature, without anyone asking him to be.

Sometimes you arrive at love before going through the first stage of attraction. The light from the window illuminated his body as he helped that sick woman and then squatted to speak to the boy and his father. After that I found myself imprinted with his face; it gazed at me in daydreams. Here it is, or was: slightly narrow, with hooded eyes and thick eyebrows over modestly stubbled cheeks, and sensual lips from which that day came words of solace so tenderhearted that I thought: *This isn't natural; he must be queer.* And indeed he was, as I found out, sitting with him in a café a week later over cups of the local mudlike coffee. He didn't realize how his kindness and his charity had pierced me until I told him about my own vulnerabilities, and the erotic directions in which I was inclined, whereupon he looked at me with an expression of amused relief. When I confessed how the sight of him had stunned me, he said, very thoughtfully, "I can help you with that," and then he put his hand on my knee so quickly that even I hardly noticed the gesture.

Being white and gay in Ethiopia is no easy matter, but we managed it by meeting on weekends in the nearest city. We'd go to multinational hotels, the impersonal expense-account Hiltons with which I am familiar and where they don't care who you are. In those days, before he got sick, Matty Quinn walked around with a lilt, his arm half-raised in a potential greeting, as if he were seeking voters. His good humor and sense made his happiness contagious. A good soul has a certain lightness and lifts up those who surround it. He lifted me. We fucked like champions and then poured wine for each other. I loved him for himself and for how he made me feel. I wonder if Jesus had that effect on people. I think so.

---

delusion idea or belief that is not true

* **compassion** *Mitleid, Mitgefühl*

to squat to bend your knees and lower yourself towards the ground

hooded eyes eyes which are partly covered by eyelids
stubble *Bartstoppel*
solace *Trost*

* **to stun sb** to shock or surprise sb

lilt a springy bouncing movement

* **contagious** *ansteckend*

By the time we both came back to the States, however, Quinn was already sick. I said I could fly out to see him, but he asked me not to, given his present condition. He was living in a friend's basement, he told me, and was looking around for a job, and he didn't want me to visit until his circumstances had improved. That was untrue, about the job. Instead, he was losing himself. He was breaking down. He was particulating. When he disappeared, I resolved to find him.

*

Entering the Inner Circle, the bar on Hennepin that I finally identified as the place that Quinn had described to me, I saw, through the tumult of louts near the entryway, a man sitting at the back of the bar, reading a book. He did not have graying black hair, but he did wear glasses, so I made my way toward him, reflexively curling my fingers into fists. I elbowed into a nearby space and ordered a beer. After waiting for a lull in the background noise and finding none, I shouted, "What's that you're reading?"

"Shakespeare!"

"Which play?"

"Not a play! The sonnets."

"Well, I'll be! When in disgrace with fortune and men's eyes!" I quoted loudly, with a calculating, companionable smile on my face. I extended my hand. "Name's Albert. Harry Albert." The man nodded but did not extend his hand in return. "Two first names? Well, I'm Blackburn."

"Black Bird?"

"No. Blackburn. Horace *Blackburn*."

"Right. My friend told me about you!"

'Who's your friend?"

"Matt Quinn."

Blackburn shook his head. "Don't know him."

"OK, you don't know him. But do you know where I might find him?"

"How could I know where he is if I don't know him?"

"Just a suspicion!" Doing business in central Africa, I had gotten used to wily characters; I was accustomed to their smug expressions of guarded cunning. They always gave themselves away by their self-amused trickster smirks. I had learned to keep pressing on these characters until they just got irritated with me.

"Come on, Mr. Blackburn," I said. "Let's not pretend. Let's get in the game here and then go to the moon, all right?"

"I don't know where he is," Blackburn insisted. I wondered how long this clown had carried on as a pseudo-Indian peddling narcotic painkillers to lowlife addicts and to upstanding citizens who then became addicts. Probably for years, maybe since childhood. And the Shakespeare! Just a bogus literary affectation. He smelled of breath mints and had a tattoo on his neck.

"However," he said slyly, "if I *were* looking for him, I'd go down to the river and I'd search for him in the shadows by the Hennepin Avenue Bridge." Blackburn then displayed an unwitting smile. "Guys like that turn into trolls, you know?" His eyes flashed. "Faggot trolls especially."

Reaching over with profound deliberation, I spilled the man's 7 Up over his edition of Shakespeare, dropped some money on the bar, and walked out. If this unregistered barroom brave wanted to follow me, I was ready. Every man should know how to throw a good punch, gay men especially. I have a remarkably quick combination of left jabs and a right uppercut, and I can take a punch without crumpling. Mine is not a glass jaw. You hit me, you hit a stone.

Outside the bar, I asked a policeman to point me in the direction of the Mississippi River, which he did with a bored, hostile stare.

I searched down there that night for Quinn, and the next night I searched for him again. For a week, I patrolled the riverbank, watching the barges pass, observing the joggers, and inhaling the pleasantly fetid river air. I kept his face before me as lovers do, a light to guide me, and like any lover I was single-minded. I spoke his name in prayer. Gradually I widened the arc of my survey to include the areas around the university and the hospitals. Many dubious characters presented themselves to me, but I am a fighter and did not fear them.

One night around 1 A.M., I was walking through one of the darkest sections along the river, shadowed even during the day by canopies of maple trees, when I saw in the deep obscurity a solitary man sitting on a park bench. I could make him out from the pinpoint reflected light from buildings on the other bank. He was barely discernible there, hardly a man at all, he had grown so thin.

Approaching him, I saw that this wreck was my beloved Matty Quinn, or what remained of him. I called his name. He turned his head toward me and gave me a look of recognition colored over with indifference. He did not rise to greet me, so I could not hug him. He emanated an odor of the river, as if he had been living in it. After I sat down next to him, I tenderly took him into my arms as if he would break. But he had al-

---

bogus fake

unwitting here: not intended, inadvertent
troll here: sb who lives in a cave
faggot (pej.) homosexual
deliberation consideration, thinking about sth carefully

Why does Harry Albert act aggressively?

barge cargo ship
fetid having a strong smell

canopy here: a mass of leaves and branches that form a cover

discernible noticeable

to emanate to emit, to spread

ready been broken. I kissed his cheek. Something terrible bad happened to him, but he recognized me; he knew me.

"I was afraid it was you Harry," he said. "I was afraid you would find me."

"Of course I would find you. I went searching."

He lifted up his head as if listening for something. "Do you think we're all being watched? Do you think anything is watching us?"

At first I thought he meant surveillance cameras, and then I understood that he was referring to the gods. "No," I said. "Nothing is ever watching us, Matty. We're all unwatched." Then I said, "I want you to come back with me. I have a hotel room. Let me feed you and clean you up and clothe you. I should never have left you alone, goddamn it. I shouldn't have let you end up back here. Come with me. Look at you. You're shivering."

"This is very sweet of you," he said. "You're admirable. But the thing is, I keep waiting for him." He did not elaborate.

"Who?"

"I keep waiting for that boy. Remember? That mother's boy? And then when he shows up, I always hit him with a baseball bat." This was pure dissociation.

"You're not making any sense," I said. "Let's go. Let's get you in the shower and wash you down and order a big steak from room service."

"No, he's *coming*," he insisted. "He'll be here any minute." And then, out of nowhere, he said, "I love you, but I'm not here now. And I won't be. Harry, give it up. Let's say goodbye."

I'm a businessman, very goal- and task-oriented, and I won't stand for talk like that. "Come on," I said. "Matty. Enough of this shit. Let's go. Let's get out of here." I stood before him and raised him by his shoulders as if he were a huge rag doll, and together, with my arm supporting him, we walked along the river road until by some miracle a taxi approached us. I hailed it, and the man drove us back to my hotel. In the lobby, the sight we presented — of a successful well-groomed gentleman holding up a shambling, smelly wreck — raised an eyebrow at the check-in desk from the night clerk, but eyebrows have never inflicted a moment of pain on me.

I bathed him that night, and I shaved him, and I ordered a cheeseburger from room service, from which he ate two bites fed from my hand to his mouth. I put him to bed in clean sheets, and all night he jabbered and shivered and cried out and tried to fight me and to escape. He actually thought he could defeat me physically, that's how deluded he was. The

dissociation here: fantasy, daydreaming

to jabber to babble

next day, after a few phone calls, I checked him into a rehab facility — they are everywhere in this region, and he was quite willing to go — and I promised to return in ten days for a visit. They don't want you sooner than that.

Matty Quinn was right: he was now a different man, his soul ruined by his dealings with Black Bird, or Blackburn, or whatever that scholar of Shakespeare was calling himself these days, and I did not love him anymore. I felt fairly certain that I had gone through a one-way gate and would not be able to love him again. I can be fickle, I admit. Yet I would not abandon him until he was ready for it. In the meantime, out of the love I had once felt for him, and which it had been my honor to possess, I resolved to kill his enabler.

The next night I lured Black Bird outside the Inner Circle. I informed him that I had brought with me a bulging packet of cash and that I would give it to him for the sake of my friend Quinn's painkilling drugs. But the cash was outside, I said, and only I could show him where. I did my best to look like a sucker.

Once in the shadows, I worked quickly and efficiently on him, and then after some minutes I left Black Bird battered on the brick pavement out of sight of the bar's alley entryway. The man was a drug dealer, and I had administered to him the beating I thought he deserved. I would have beaten Matty's doctor too, the one who first prescribed the painkillers, but they don't let you do that; you can't assault our medical professionals. Black Bird had gotten the brunt of it. But the angel of justice calls for retribution in kind, and since Matty Quinn was still alive, so, in his way, was Black Bird.

When Matty was ready to be discharged, I returned to Minneapolis and picked him up. Imagine this: the sun was blazing, and in broad daylight the man I had once loved folded himself up into my slate-gray rental car, and we drove like any old couple to the basement where he had been staying. We picked up his worldly possessions, the ones he wished to keep and to take with him to Seattle. Remnants: a high school yearbook, photographs of the village where he had worked in Ethiopia, a pair of cuff links, a clock radio, a laptop computer, a few books, and clothes, including a dark blue ascot. Not loving him, I helped him pack, and, not loving him, I bought him a ticket back to Seattle.

Saying very little, we sat together on the plane, touching hands occasionally. Not loving him, I moved him temporarily into my condo and took him around Seattle and showed him how to use its public transportation system and located a job for him in a deli. Together we found him a twelve-step program for drug addicts in recovery.

He lives nearby in an apartment I hunted down for him, and we have gone on with our lives. I call him almost every night, whether I am here or away on business. Slowly, he is taking charge of his life. It seems a shame to say so, but because the light in his soul is diminished, the one in mine, out of sympathy, is diminished too. I cry occasionally, but unsentimentally, and we still take pleasure in bickering, as we always have. His inflammations still cause him pain, and he moves now with small steps like an old man, but when I am in town I bring him dinners from Trader Joe's and magazines from the drugstore, and one night he brought over a sandwich for me that he himself had made at the deli. As I bit into the rye bread and corned beef, he watched me. "You like it?" he asked.

"It's fine," I said, shrugging. "Sauerkraut's a bit thick."

"That's how I do it," he said crossly, full of rehab righteousness.

"And I like more Russian dressing than this." I glanced out the window. "Moon's out," I said. "Full, I think. Werewolf weather."

He looked at it. "You never see the moon," he said, "until you sit all night watching it and you see how blindly stupid and oafish it is. I used to talk to it. My whole autobiography. Looked like the same moon I saw in Africa, but it wasn't. Never said a damn word in return once I was here. Over there, it wouldn't shut up."

"Well, it doesn't have anything to say to Americans," I remarked, my mouth full. "We're beyond that. Anything on TV?"

"Yeah," he said, "junkie TV, where people are about to die from their failings. Then they're rescued by Dr. Phil and put on the boat to that enchanted island they have." He waited. I got the feeling that he didn't believe in his own recovery. Or in the American project. Maybe we weren't really out of the woods.

"OK, here's what I want you to do," he said. "I want you to call up Benny Takemitsu and tell him that I owe him some money." He laughed at the joke. Even his eyes lit up at the prankster aspect of making amends and its bourgeois comforts. "Tell him I'll pay him eventually. I'll pay him ten cents on the dollar."

"That's a good one."

"Hey, even Plato was disappointed by the material world. Me too."

"Gotcha."

to bicker to argue

oafish clumsy and stupid

enchanted bewitched, under the influence of charms or spells

prankster sb who plays tricks on other people
to make amends to compensate for doing sth wrong
bourgeois (pej.) here: concerned about money and material wealth

* to pour sb a drink *jmdm. ein Getränk einschenken*

to upend sth to turn sth upside down

"Pour me a drink," he commanded. I thought I knew what he was going to do, so I gave him what he wanted, some scotch with ice, despite my misgivings.

"Here's how you do it," he said, when he had the scotch in his hand. "Remember what they did in Ethiopia, that ceremonial thing?" He slowly upended the drink and emptied it out on my floor, where it puddled on the dining room tile. "In memory of those who are gone. In memory of those down below us."

It felt like a toast to our former selves. I looked out at the silent moon, imagining for a moment that he would be all right after all, and then I remembered to follow along. You're supposed to do it outside, on the ground, not in a building, but I inverted my beer bottle anyway. The beer gurgled out onto the dining room floor, and I smiled as if something true and actual had happened, this import-ritual. Quinn smiled back, triumphant.

The Best American Short Stories 2014. Eds. Jennifer Egan, Heidi Pitlor. New York: Houghton Mifflin Harcourt, 2014, pp. 1 – 14.

About My Aunt
Joan Silber

This happens a lot — people travel and they find places they like so much, they think they've risen to their best selves just by being there. They feel distant from everyone at home who can't begin to understand. If they're young, they take up with beautiful locals of the opposite sex; they settle in; they get used to how everything works; they make homes. But usually not forever.

I had an aunt who was such a person. She went to Istanbul when she was in her twenties. She met a good-looking carpet seller from Cappadocia. She'd been a classics major in college and had many questions to ask him, many observations to offer. He was a gentle and intelligent man who spent his days talking to travelers. He'd come to think he no longer knew what to say to Turkish girls, and he loved my aunt's airy conversation. When her girlfriends went back to Greece, she stayed behind and moved in with him. This was in 1970.

His shop was in Sultanahmet, a well-touristed part of the city, and he lived in Fener, an old and jumbled neighborhood. Kiki, my aunt, liked having people over, and their apartment was always filled with men from her husband's region and expats of various ages. She was happy to cook big semi-Turkish meals and make up the couch for anyone passing through. She helped out in the store, explained carpet motifs to anyone who walked in — those were stars for happiness; scorpion designs to keep real scorpions away. In her letters home, she sounded enormously pleased with herself — she dropped Turkish phrases into her sentences, reported days spent sipping *çay* and *kahve*. She sent home to Brooklyn a carpet she said was Kurdish.

Then Kiki's boyfriend's business took a turn for the worse. There was a flood in the basement of his store and a bill someone never paid and a new shop nearby that was getting all the business. Or something. The store had to close. Her family thought this meant that Kiki was coming home at last. But no. Osman, her guy, had decided to move back to his village to help his father, who raised pumpkins for their seed oil, as well as tomatoes, green squash, and eggplant. Kiki was up for the move; she wanted to see the real Turkey. Istanbul was really so Western now. Cappadocia was very ancient and she couldn't wait to see the volcanic rock. She was getting married! Her family in Brooklyn was surprised about that part. Were they

---

Cappadocia a region in Central Anatolia
★ **classics** the languages and cultures of Greek and Roman antiquity
★ **major** here: *Hauptfachstudent*
airy proud and haughty

jumbled disorderly

expat (infml.) expatriate, i. e. sb who lives outside their country of origin

çay, kahve (Turk.) tea, coffee

squash *Kürbis*
eggplant *Aubergine*

invited to the wedding? Apparently not. In fact, it had probably happened already by the time they got the letter. "Wearing a beaded hat and a glitzy head scarf, the whole shebang," Kiki wrote. "I still can't believe it."

Neither could any of her relatives. But they sent presents, once they had an address. A microwave oven, a Mr. Coffee, an electric blanket for the cold mountains. They were a practical and liberal family; they wanted to be helpful. "I know it's hard for you to imagine," Kiki wrote, "but we do very well without electricity here. Every morning I make a wood fire in the stove. Very good-smelling smoke. I make a little fire in the bottom of the water heater too."

Kiki built fires? No one could imagine her as the pioneer wife. Her brother, Alan (who later became my father), was always hoping to visit. Kiki said not a word about making any visits home. No one nagged her; she'd been a touchy teenager, given to sullen outbursts, and everyone was afraid of that Kiki appearing again.

She stayed for eight years. Her letters said, "My husband thinks I sew as well as his sisters" and "I'm rereading my copy of Ovid in Latin. It's not bad!" and "Winter sooo long this year, I hate it. Osman has already taught me all he knows about the stars." No one could make sense of who she was now. There were no children and no pregnancies that anyone heard about, and the family avoided asking.

Her brother was just about to finally get himself over for a visit when Kiki wrote to say, "Guess what? I'm coming back at last. For good." No, the husband was not coming with her. "My life here has reached its natural conclusion," Kiki wrote. "Osman will be my dear friend forever but we've come to the end of our road."

"So who ran around on who?" the relatives kept asking. "She'll never say, will she?"

Everybody wondered what she would look like when she returned. Would she be sun-dried and weather-beaten, would she wear billowing silk trousers like a belly dancer's, would the newer buildings of New York amaze her? None of the above. She looked like the same old Kiki, thirty-one with very good skin, and she was wearing jeans and a turtleneck, possibly the same ones she'd left home with.

Her luggage was a mess, woven plastic valises baled up with string, very third world, and there were a lot of them. She had brought back nine carpets! What was she thinking? She intended to sell them.

Her brother always remembered that when they ate their first meal together, Kiki held her knife and fork like a European. She laughed at things lightly, as if the absurdity of it all wasn't worth shrieking over. She teased Alan about his eyeglasses ("you look like a genius in them") and his large appetite ("has not changed since you were eight"). She certainly sounded like herself.

Before very long, she moved in with someone named Marcy she'd known at Brooklyn College. Marcy's mother bought the biggest of the rugs, and Kiki used the proceeds to rent a storefront in the East Village where she displayed her carpets and other items she had brought back — a brass tea set and turquoise beads and cotton pants with tucked hems that she herself had once worn.

The store stayed afloat for a while. Her brother wondered if she was dealing drugs — hashish was all over Istanbul in the movie *Midnight Express*, which had come out just before her return. Kiki refused to see such a film, with its lurid scenes of mean Turkish prisons. "Who has *nice* prisons?" she said. "Name one single country in the world. Just one."

When her store began to fail and she had to give it up, Kiki supported herself by cleaning houses. She evidently did this with a good spirit; the family was much more embarrassed about it than she was. "People here don't know *how* to clean their houses," she would say. "It's sort of remarkable, isn't it?"

*

By the time I was a little kid, Kiki had become the assistant director of a small agency that booked housekeepers and nannies. She was the one you got on the phone, the one who didn't take any nonsense from clients or workers either. She was friendly but strict and kept people on point.

As a child I was a teeny bit afraid of her. She could be very withering if I was acting up and getting crazy and knocking over chairs. But when my parents took me to visit, Kiki had special cookies for me (I loved Mallomars) and for a while she had a boyfriend named Hernando who would play airplane with me and go buzzing around the room with me on his back. I loved visiting her.

My father told me later that Hernando had wanted to marry Kiki. "But she wasn't made for marriage," he said. "Its not all roses, you know." He and my mother had a history of having, as they say, their differences.

"Kiki was always like a bird," my father said. "Flying here and there."

What a corny thing to say.

---

to shriek to yell, to scream

proceeds (pl.) profit

to tuck sth *etw. stecken (z. B. Kleidung)*
hem *Saum*

lurid here: shocking, causing revulsion

corny *kitschig*

to spurn sth to reject sth, to scorn sth
disdain contempt

★ **to be on good terms** gut miteinander auskommen

Hurricane Sandy
One of the most destructive hurricanes in US history, Hurricane Sandy hit the eastern seaboard in October 2012, killing 233 people. Damages were particularly severe in the states of New Jersey and New York. Large parts of New York City were affected by power outages.

tint Farbton

awning Markise

★ **(TV) coverage** (TV-) Berichterstattung
Con Ed Consolidated Edison Inc., a large US energy company

I grew up outside Boston, in a small suburban town, whose leafy safety I spurned once I was old enough for hip disdain. I moved to New York as soon as I finished high school, which I barely did. My parents and I were not on good terms in my early years in the city, but Kiki made a point of keeping in touch. She'd call on the phone and say, "I'm thirsty, let's go have a drink. OK?" At first I was up in Inwood, as far north in Manhattan as you can get, so it was a long subway ride to see her in the East Village, but once I moved to Harlem it wasn't quite so bad. When my son was born, four years ago, Kiki brought me the most useful baby stuff, things a person couldn't even know she needed. Oliver would calm down and sleep when she walked him around. He grew up calling her Aunt Great Kiki.

The two of us lived in a housing project, but one of the nicer ones, in an apartment illegally passed on to me by an ex-boyfriend. It was a decent size, with good light, and I liked my neighbors. That fall the TV started telling us to get prepared for Hurricane Sandy, and Oliver had a great time flicking the flashlight on and off (a really annoying game) and watching me tape giant X's on the window glass. All the kids on our floor were hyped up and excited, running around and shrieking. We kept looking out the windows as the sky turned a sepia tint. When the rains broke and began to come down hard, we could hear the moaning of the winds and things clattering and banging in the night, awnings and trees getting the hell beaten out of them. I kept switching to different channels on the TV so we wouldn't miss any of it. The television had better coverage than my view out the window. A newscaster in a suit told us the Con Ed transformer on Fourteenth Street exploded! The lights in the bottom of Manhattan had gone out! I made efforts to explain electricity to Oliver, as if I knew. Never, never put your finger in a socket. Oliver wanted to watch a better program.

At nine-thirty my father called to say, "Your aunt Kiki doesn't have power, you know. She's probably sitting in the dark." I had forgotten about her entirely. She was on East Fifth Street, in the no-electricity zone. I promised I'd check on Kiki in the morning.

"I might have to walk there," I said. "It's like a hundred and twenty blocks. You're not going to ask about my neighborhood? It's fine."

"Don't forget about her, OK? Promise me that."

"I just told you," I said.

The next day the weather was shockingly pleasant, mild, with a white sky. We walked for a half-hour, which Oliver really did not like, past some downed trees and tossed branches, and then a cab miraculously stopped and we shared it with an old guy all the way downtown. No traffic lights working, no stores open — how strange the streets were. In Kiki's building, I led Oliver up four flights of dark tenement stairs while he drove me nuts flicking the flashlight on and off.

When Kiki opened the door onto her pitch-black hallway, she said, "Reyna! What are you doing here?"

Kiki, of course, was fine. She had plenty of vegetables and canned food and rice — who needed a fridge? — and she could light the stove with a match. She had daylight now and candles for later. She had pots of water she could boil to wash with. She had filled the tub the night before. How was *I*? "Oliver, isn't this fun?" she said.

Oh, New Yorkers were making such a big fuss, she thought. She had a transistor radio so the fussing came through. "I myself am enjoying the day off from work," she said. She was rereading *The Greek Way* by Edith Hamilton — had I ever read it? I didn't read much, did I? — and she planned to finish it tonight by candlelight.

"Come stay with us," I said. "Wouldn't you like that, Oliver?" Oliver crowed on cue.

Kiki said she always preferred being in her own home. "Oliver, I bet you would like some of the chocolate ice cream that's turning into a lovely milk shake."

We followed her into the kitchen, with its painted cabinets and old linoleum. When I took off my jacket to settle in, Kiki said, "Oh, no. Did you get a new tattoo?"

"*No*. You always ask that. You're phobic about my arms."

"I'll never get used to them."

I had a dove and a sparrow and a tiger lily and a branch with leaves and some small older ones. They all stood for things. The dove was to settle a fight; the sparrow was the true New York bird; the tiger lily meant boldness; and the branch was an olive tree in honor of Oliver. I used to try to tell Kiki that they were no different from the patterns on rugs. "Are you a floor?" she said. She accused my tattoos of being forms of mutilation as well as forms of deception over my natural skin. According to what? "Well, Islamic teaching, for one thing," she said.

Kiki had never been a practicing Muslim but she liked a lot about Islam. I may have been the only one in the family who knew how into it she'd once been. She used to try to get me to read Averroës, she thought he was great, and Avicenna. Only

flight here: stairs from one floor of a building to another
tenement cheap building containing several flats with just the minimum standard of quality

to make a fuss *sich anstellen*

★ **on cue** at exactly the right moment

★ **boldness** courage, bravery

★ **mutilation** *Verstümmelung*

★ **deception** *Täuschung*
deceit (no pl.) *Täuschung, Betrug*
deceitful(ly) *hinterlistig*
to deceive sb *jmdn. betrügen, täuschen*
deceiver *Betrüger*

my aunt would believe that someone like me could just dip into twelfth-century philosophy if I felt like it. She saw no reason why not.

"Oliver, my man," she was saying now, "you don't have to finish if you're full."

"Dad's worried about you," I told Kiki.

"I already called him," she said. It turned out her phone still worked because she had an old landline, nothing digital or bundled.

She'd been outside earlier in the day. Some people on her block had water but she didn't. Oliver was entranced when Kiki showed him how she flushed the toilet by throwing down a potful of water.

"It's magic," I said.

When we left, Kiki called after us, "I'm always glad to see you, you know that." She could have given us more credit for getting all the way there, I thought.

'You might change your mind about staying with us," I called back, before we went out into the dark hall.

I had an extra reason for wanting her to stay. Not to be one of those mothers who was always desperate for babysitting, but I needed a babysitter.

My boyfriend, Boyd, was spending three months at Rikers Island. He was there for selling five ounces of weed (who thinks that should even be a crime?). For all of October I'd gone to see him once a week, and it made a big difference to him. I planned to go that week, once the subways were running and buses were going over the bridge again. But it was hard bringing Oliver, who wasn't his kid and who needed a lot of attention during those toyless visits.

I loved Boyd but I wouldn't have said I loved him more than the others I'd been with. Fortunately no one asked. Not even Boyd. There was no need for people to keep mouthing off about how much they felt, in his view. Some degree of real interest, some persistence in showing up, was enough. Every week I saw him sitting in that visitors' room in his stupid jumpsuit. The sight of him — heavy-faced, wary, waiting to smile slightly — always got to me, and when I hugged him (light hugs were permitted), I'd think, *It's still Boyd, it's Boyd here.*

Oliver could be a nuisance. Sometimes he was very, very whiny after standing in so many different lines, or he was incensed that he couldn't bring in his giant plastic dinosaur. Or he got overstimulated and had to nestle up to Boyd and complain at length about some kid who threw sand in the park. "You having adventures, right?" Boyd said. Meanwhile, I was trying to ask Boyd if he'd had an OK week and why not. I had an hour to give him the joys of my conversation. Dealing with those two at once was not the easiest.

> ⬆ What is the relationship between Boyd and Reyna, the narrator?

I got a phone call from Aunt Kiki on the second day after the hurricane. "How would you feel about my coming over after work to take a hot shower?" she said. "I can bring a towel, I've got piles of towels."

"Our shower is dying to see you," I said. "And Oliver will lend you his ducky."

"Kiki Kiki Kiki Kiki Kiki!" Oliver yelled when she came through the door. Maybe I'd worked him up too much in advance. We'd gotten the place very clean.

As soon as my aunt emerged from the bathroom, dressed again in her slacks and sweater and with a steamed-pink face under the turban of her towel, I handed her a glass of red wine. "A person without heat or water needs alcohol," I said. We sat down to meatloaf, which I was good at, and mashed potatoes with garlic, which Oliver had learned to eat.

> **slacks** (pl.) trousers
>
> **meatloaf** Hackbraten

"This is a feast," she said. "Did you know the sultans had feasts that went on for two weeks?"

Oliver was impressed. "This one could go on longer," I said. "You should stay over. Or come back tomorrow. I mean it."

Tomorrow was what I needed — it was the visiting night for inmates with last names from *M* to *Z*.

"Maybe the power will be back on by then," Kiki said. "Maybe maybe."

> ★ **inmate** sb who is kept in a prison, a mental hospital, etc.

At Rikers, Boyd and the other inmates had spent the hurricane under lockdown, no wandering off into the torrent. Rikers had its own generator, and the buildings were in the center of the island, too high up to wash away. It was never meant to be a place you might swim from.

> **torrent** fast and powerful flow of water

"You know I have this boyfriend, Boyd," I said.

Kiki was looking at her plate while I told her, as much as I could in front of Oliver, the situation about the weekly visits. "Oh, shit," she said. She had to finish chewing to say, "OK, sure, OK, I'll come right from work."

When I leaned over to embrace her, she seemed embarrassed "Oh, please," she said. "No big deal."

What a mystery Kiki was. What could I ever say to her that would throw her for a loop? Best not to push it, of course. And

> **to throw sb for a loop** to completely surprise sb

maybe she had a boyfriend of her own that I didn't even know about. She wasn't someone who told you everything. She wasn't showering with him, wherever he was. Maybe he was married. A man that age. Oh, where was I going with this? When Kiki turned up the next night, she was forty-five minutes later than she'd said she'd be, and I had given up on her several times over. She bustled through the door, saying, "Don't ask me how the subways are running. Go, go. Get out of here, go."

flushed looking slightly red; full of life and energy

She looked younger, all flushed like that. What a babe she must've once been. Or at least a hippie sweetheart. Oliver clambered all over her. "Will you hurry up and get out of here?" she said to me.

The subway (which had only started running that day) was indeed slow to arrive and very crowded, but the bus near Queens Plaza that went to Rikers was the same as ever. After the first few stops, all the white people except me emptied out. I read *People* magazine while we inched our way to the bridge to the island; love was making a mess of the lives of a number of celebrities. And look at that teenage girl across the aisle in the bus, combing her hair, checking it in a mirror, pulling some strands across her face to make it hang right. *Girl,* I wanted to say, *he fucked up bad enough to get himself where he is, and you're still worried he won't like your hair?*

mousse here: *Haarfestiger*

Of course, I was all moussed and lipsticked myself. I had standards. But you couldn't wear anything too revealing — rips or see-through fabrics — they had rules. *Visitors must wear undergarments.*

After I stood in a line and put my coat and purse in a locker and showed my ID to the guards and got searched and stood in a line for one of Rikers' own buses and got searched again, I sat in a room to wait for Boyd. It was odd being there without Oliver. The wait went on so long, and it wasn't like you could bring a book. And then I heard Boyd's name read from the list.

Those jumpsuits didn't flatter anyone. But when we hugged, he smelled of soap and Boyd, and I was sorry for myself to have him away so long. "Hey there," he said.

"Didn't mean to get here so late," I said.

Boyd wanted to hear about the hurricane and who got hit the worst. Aunt Kiki became my material: "Oh, she had her candles and her pots of water and her cans of soup and her bags of rice, she couldn't see why everybody was so upset."

"Can't keep 'em down, old people like that," he said. "Good for her. That's the best thing I've heard all week."

I went on about Kiki's gameness. How she'd taught me the right way to climb trees when I was young, when my mother only worried I'd fall on my head.

"I didn't know you were a climber. Have to tell Claude."

His friend Claude, much more of an athlete than Boyd, had recently discovered the climbing wall at some gym. Boyd himself was a couch potato, but a lean and lanky one. People told him he looked like LeBron James, only skinnier. Was he getting puffy now? A little.

"Claude's a monster on that wall. Got Lynnette doing it too." Lynnette was Claude's sister. And Boyd's girlfriend before me.

"Girls can do that stuff fine, he says."

"When did he say that?"

"They came by last week. The whole gang."

What gang? Only three visitors allowed. "Lynnette was here?"

"And Maxwell. They came to show support. I appreciated it, you know?"

I'll bet you did, I thought. I was trying not to leap to any conclusions. It wasn't as if she could've crept into the corner with him for a quickie, though you heard rumors of such things. Urban myths.

"Does Claude still have that stringy haircut?"

"He does. Looks like a root vegetable. Man should go to my barber." The Rikers barber had given Boyd an onion look, if you were citing vegetables.

"They're coming again Saturday. You're not coming Saturday, right?"

I never came on Saturdays. I cut him a look.

"Because if you are," he said, "I'll tell them not to come."

You couldn't blame a man who had nothing for wanting everything he could get his hands on. This was pretty much what I thought on the bus ride back to the subway. Oh, I could blame him. I was spending an hour and a half to get there every week and an hour and a half to get back so he could entertain his ex? I was torn between being pissed off and my principles about being a good sport. Why had Boyd told me? The guy could keep his mouth shut when he needed to.

Because he didn't think he needed to. Because I was a good sport. What surprised me even more was how painful this was starting to be. I could imagine Boyd greeting Lynnette, in his offhand, Mr. Cool Way. "Can I believe my eyes?" Lynnette silky and tough, telling him it had been too long. But what was so great about Boyd that I should twist in torment from what I was seeing too clearly in my head?

---

gameness courage

lanky schlaksig
puffy aufgedunsen

LeBron James (★1984), one of the most successful American basketball players of his generation. He won several NBA Championships, NBA Most Valuable Player Awards and two Olympic gold medals.

torment suffering, pain

I was on the bus during this anguish. I wanted Boyd to comfort me. He had a talent for that. If you were insulted because some asshole at daycare said your kid's shoes were unsuitable, if you splurged on a nice TV and then realized you'd overpaid, if you got fired from your job because you used up sick days and it wasn't your fault, Boyd could make it seem hilarious. He could remind you it was part of the ever-expanding joke of human trouble. Not just you.

When I got back to the apartment, Oliver was actually asleep in his bed — had Kiki drugged him? — and Kiki was in the living room watching the Cooking Channel on TV.
"You watch this crap?" I said.
"How was the visit?"
"Medium. Who's winning on *Chopped*?"
"The wrong guy. But I have a thing for Marcus Samuelsson." He was the judge who had a restaurant right in Harlem, a chef born in Ethiopia, tall and rangy and very good-looking. So, I wanted to ask Kiki and I almost did, *is the whole fucking world about men?*
"Oliver spilled a lot of yogurt on the floor but we got it cleaned up," she said.
I wanted a drink, I wanted a joint. What was in the house? I found a very old bottle of Beaujolais in the kitchen and poured glasses for us both.
"When does he get out?" Kiki asked.
"They say January. He's holding up OK."
"He has you."
"You don't have to tell me if you don't want to, but when you got divorced," I said, "was it because one of you had been messing around with someone else?"
"Whooh," Kiki said, "where did that come from?"
"Someone named Lynnette has been visiting Boyd."
Kiki considered this. "Could be nothing."
"So when you left Turkey, why did you leave?"
"It was time."
I admired Kiki's way of deciding what was none of your business, but it made you think there was business there.

It was my bad luck that Con Ed got its act together the very next evening, so electricity flowed in the walls of Kiki's home to give her light and refrigeration and to pump her water and the gurgling steam in her radiators. I called her to say Happy Normal.
"Normal is overrated," she said, "I'll be so busy next week."
"Me too," I said.

---

to splurge to spend a lot of money

Marcus Samuelsson (*1971), a renowned New York-based chef, cookbook author and TV personality. He was born in Ethiopia and raised in Sweden.

Oliver hardly ever had sitters. He was in daycare while I went off to my unglamorous employment as a part-time receptionist at a veterinarian's office (it paid lousy but the dogs were usually nice) and at night I took him with me if I went to see friends or Boyd, when I used to stay with Boyd. Sometimes Boyd had a cousin who watched him.

"Oliver wants to say hi," I told my aunt.

"I *love* you, Great Kiki!" Oliver said.

This didn't move her to volunteer to sit for him another time, and I thought it was better not to ask again so soon.

Oliver wasn't bad at all on the next visit to Rikers. The weather was colder and he got to wear his favorite Spider-Man sweater, which Boyd said was very sharp.

"Your mom's looking good too," Boyd said to Oliver.

"Better than Lynnette?"

I hadn't meant to say any such whiny-bitch thing; it leaped out of me. I was horrified. I wasn't as good as I thought I was, was I?

"Not in your league," Boyd said. "Girl's nowhere near." He said this slowly and soberly. He shook his onion head for emphasis.

The rest of the visit went very well. Boyd suggested that Oliver now had the superpower to spin webs from the ceiling — "You going to float above us all, land right on all the bad guys" – and Oliver was so tickled he had to be stopped from shrieking with glee at top volume.

"Know what I miss?" Boyd said. "Well, that, of course. Don't look at me that way. But also I miss when we used to go ice skating."

We had gone exactly twice, renting skates in Central Park, falling on our asses. I almost crushed Oliver one time I went down. "You telling everyone you're the next big hockey star?" I said.

"I hope there's still ice when I get out," he said.

"There will be," I said. "It's soon. Before you know it."

Kiki had now started to worry about me; she called more often than I was used to. She'd say, "You think Obama's going to get this Congress in line? And how's Boyd doing?"

I let her know we were still an item, which was what she wanted to know. Why in God's name would I ever think of splitting up with Boyd before I could at least get him back home and in bed again? What was the point of all these bus rides if I was going to skip that part?

tickled here: delighted
to shriek with glee *vor Freude jauchzen*

"You wouldn't want me to desert him at a time like this," I said.
"Be careful," she said.
"He's not much of a criminal," I said. "He was just a bartender selling on the side, not any big-time guy." I didn't have to tell her not to mention this to my father.
"Anybody can be in jail, I know that," Kiki said. "'Hikmet was in jail for thirteen years in Turkey."
I thought she meant an old flame of hers but it turned out she meant a famous poet who was dead before she even got there. A famous Communist poet. She'd read all his prison poems. Boyd wasn't in jail for politics, although some people claimed the war on drugs was a race war, and they had a point. My mom and dad were known to smoke dope every now and then, and was any cop stop-and-frisking them on the streets of Brookline?
"So can I ask you," I said, "were there drugs around when you were in Turkey?" What a blurter I was these days. "Were people selling hash or anything?"
"Not in our circles. I hate that movie, you've seen that movie. But there was smuggling. I mean in antiquities, bits from ancient sites. People went across to the eastern parts, brought stuff back. Or they got it over the border from Iran. Beautiful things, really."
"It's amazing what people get money for."
"If Osman had wanted to do that," she said, "he wouldn't have become a farmer. It was the farming that made me leave, by the way."
I was very pleased that she told me.
"And he left off farming five years later," she said. "Isn't that ironic?"
"It is," I said.
"I still write to Osman. He's a great letter writer."
This was news. Did she have all the letters; how hot were they; did he e-mail too? Of course, I was thinking: *Maybe you two should get back together.* It's a human impulse, isn't it, to want to set the world into couples.
"The wife he has now is much younger," Kiki said.

By December I'd gotten a new tattoo in honor of Boyd's impending release. It was quite beautiful — a birdcage with the door open and a line of tiny birds going toward my wrist. Some people design their body art so it all fits together, but I did mine piecemeal, like my life, and it looked fine.
Kiki noticed it when it was a week old and still swollen. She had just made supper for us (overcooked hamburgers but Oli-

ver liked them) and I was doing the dishes, keeping that arm out of the water. Soaking too soon was bad for it.
"And when Boyd is out of the picture," Kiki said, "you'll be stuck with this ink that won't go away."
"It's my history," I said. "My arm is an album."
"What if Boyd doesn't like it?"
"It's for *me*," I said. "All of these are *mine*."
"Don't be a carpet," she said.
"You don't really know very much about this," I said, "if you don't mind my saying."
Why would I take advice from a woman who slept every night alone in her bed, cuddling up with some copy of Aristotle? What could she possibly tell me that I could use? And she was getting older by the minute, with her squinty eyes and her short hair cut too close to her head.

It was snowing the day Boyd got released from Rikers. I was home with Oliver when Claude went to pick him up. He didn't want me and Oliver seeing him then, with his bag of items, with his humbling paperwork, with the guards leaning over every detail. By the time I got to view Boyd he was in our local coffee shop with Claude, eating a cheeseburger, looking happy and greasy. Oliver went berserk, leaping all over him, smearing his snowy boots all over Boyd's pants. I leaped a little too. "Don't knock me over," Boyd said. "Nah, knock me over. Go ahead."
"Show him no mercy," Claude said.
Already Boyd looked vastly better than he had in jail, and he'd been out only an hour. "Can't believe it," he said. "Can't believe I was ever there." He fed french fries to Oliver, who pretended to be a dog. Boyd had his other hand on my knee. We could do that now. "Hey, girl," he said. The snow outside the window gave everything a lunar brightness.

The first night he stayed with me, after it took forever to get Oliver asleep in the other room, I was madly eager when we made our way to each other at last. How did it go, this dream — did we still know how to do this? Knew just fine, though there were fumbles and pauses, little laughing hesitations. I had imagined Boyd would be hungry and even rough, but no, he was careful; he looped around and circled back and took some byways before settling on his goal. He was trying, it seemed to me, to make this first contact very particular, trying to recognize me. I hadn't expected this from him, which showed what I knew.

squinty looking with eyes partly closed

Aristotle (384–322 BC) was a Greek philosopher. A disciple of Plato, he was the first to establish a system of Western philosophy and instrumental in shaping the method of empiricism.

greasy (pej.) schmierig

At my job in the vet's office my fellow workers teased me about being sleepy at the desk. They all knew my boyfriend had returned after a long trip. Any yawn brought on group hilarity. "Look how she walks, she hobbles," one of the techs said. What a raunchy office I worked in. All I said was, "Laugh away, you're green with envy."

I was distracted, full of wayward thoughts — Boyd and I starting a restaurant together, Boyd and I running off to Thailand, Boyd and I having another kid, maybe a girl, what would we name her, Oliver would like this — or would he? I lost focus while I was doing my tasks at the computer and had to put up with everyone saying how sleepy I was.

Jail doesn't always change people in good ways, but in Boyd's case it made him quieter and less apt to throw his weight around. He had to find a new job (no alcohol). I was proud of him when he started as a waiter in a diner just north of our neighborhood, a big challenge to his stylish self. This was definitely a step down for him, which he bore grudgingly but not bitterly. After work his hair smelled of frying oil and broiler smoke. His home was not exactly with me — he was officially living at his cousin's, since he no longer had his apartment — but he spent a lot of nights at my place. I liked the cousin (it was Maxwell, who had once babysat for Oliver) but he had a tendency to drag Boyd out to clubs at night. In my younger days I liked to go clubbing same as anyone, but once I had Oliver it pretty much lost its appeal. I had reason to imagine girls in teensy outfits throwing themselves at Boyd in these clubs, but it turned out that wasn't the problem. The problem was that Maxwell had a scheme for increasing Boyd's admittedly paltry income. It had to do with smuggling cigarettes from Virginia to New York, of all idiotic ways to make a profit. Just to cash in on the tax difference. "Are you out of your fucking mind?" I said. "You want to violate probation?"

"Don't shout," Boyd said.

"Crossing state lines. Are you crazy?"

"That's it," Boyd said. "No more talking. You always have opinions. Topic closed. Forget I said a word."

I didn't take well to being shushed. I snapped at him and he got stony and went home early that night. "A man needs peace, is that too much to ask?"

"You think I give a fuck?" I said.

I was with Kiki the next day, having lunch near my office. She was checking up on me these days as much as she could, which included treating me to a falafel plate. I told her about the dog I'd met at my job who knew three languages. It could sit, lie down, and beg in English, Spanish, and ASL. "A pit-bull mix. They're smart."

"You know what I think?" Kiki said. "I think you should go live somewhere where you'd learn another language. Everyone should, really."

"Someday," I said.

"I still have a friend in Istanbul. I bet you and Oliver could go camp out at her place. For a little while. It's a very kid-friendly culture."

"I don't think so. My life is here."

"It doesn't have to be Istanbul, that was my place, it's not everyone's. There are other places. I'd stake you with some cash if you wanted to take off for a while."

I wasn't even tempted.

"It's very good of you," I said.

"You'll be sorry later if you don't do it," she said.

She wanted to get me away from Boyd, which might happen on its own, anyway. I was touched and insulted both at once. And then I was trying to imagine myself in a new city. Taking Oliver to a park in Rome. Having interesting chats with the locals while I sat on a bench. Laughing away in Italian.

My phone interrupted us with the ping that meant I was getting a text. "Sorry," I said to Kiki. "I just need to check." It was Boyd, and I was so excited that I said, "Oh! From Boyd!" out loud. *Sorry, baby* was in the message, and some other things that I certainly wasn't reading to Kiki. But I chuckled in joy, tickled to death — I could feel myself getting flushed. How funny he could be when he wanted. That Boyd.

"Excuse me," I said. "I just have to answer fast."

"Go ahead," Kiki said, not pleasantly.

I had to concentrate to tap the letters. It took a few minutes and I could hear Kiki sigh across from me. I knew how I looked, too girly, too jacked up over crumbs Boyd threw my way. Kiki was not glad about it. She didn't even know Boyd. But I did — I could see him very distinctly in my mind just then, his grumbling sweetness, his spells of cold scorn, his bragging, his ridiculous illusions about what he could do, and the waves of tenderness I had for him, the sudden pangs of adoration. I was perfectly aware (or just then I was, anyway) that some part of my life with Boyd was not entirely real, that if I pushed it too hard a whole other feeling would show itself. I wasn't about to push. I wanted us to go on as we were. A person can know several things at once. I could know all of them while still being moved to delight by him — his kisses on my neck,

ASL (abbrev.) American Sign Language

to take off (infml.) to leave

to chuckle to laugh quietly
flushed *rot im Gesicht*

to brag to boast, to show off

his way of humming to the most blaring tune, his goofing around with Oliver. And I saw that I was probably going to help him with the cigarette smuggling too. I was going to be in it with him before I even meant to be.

I was going to ride in the car and count the cash; I was going to let him store his illegal cigarettes in my house. All because of what stirred me, all because of what Boyd was to me. All because of beauty.

I had my own life to live. And what did Kiki have? She had her job making deals between the very rich and the very poor. She had her books that she settled inside of in dusty private satisfaction. She had her old and fabled past. I loved my aunt, but she must have known I'd never listen to her.

When I stopped texting Boyd, I looked up, and Kiki was dabbing at her plate of food. "The hummus was good," I said. "They say Saladin ate hummus," she said. In the eleven hundreds. You know about him, right? He was a Kurd who fought against the Crusaders."

She knew a lot. She was waiting for me to make some fucking effort to know a fraction as much. Saladin who? In the meantime — anyone looking at our table could've seen this — we were having a long and unavoidable moment, my aunt and I, of each feeling sorry for the other. In our separate ways. How could we not?

First published in Tin House, vol. 15, no. 4. Copyright © 2014 by Joan Silber. Reprinted by permission of Joan Silber.

Con-Texts

About the authors
Ernest Hemingway (1899 – 1961)

Born on July 21, 1899, in Oak Park, Illinois, Ernest Miller Hemingway briefly worked as a journalist in Kansas City before moving to Europe. He joined the Italian forces as an ambulance driver in 1918. Recovering from a war injury, Hemingway returned to the United States where he met his first wife. They relocated to Paris, where Hemingway worked as a correspondent for the *Toronto Star*. It was in the 1920s when Hemingway launched his career as a writer. In Paris he met the likes of Pablo Picasso, James Joyce, Ezra Pound and F. Scott Fitzgerald and became part of a group of expatriate writers who were famously called the "Lost Generation", a term coined by Gertrude Stein and popularized by Hemingway in his first novel *The Sun Also Rises* (1926). His experiences of World War I were fictionalized in his novel *A Farewell to Arms* (1929), which earned him lasting critical acclaim. Hemingway was a prolific writer of short stories, too, publishing several collections. Following his novel *The Old Man and the Sea* (1952), Hemingway was awarded the Pulitzer Prize for Fiction in 1953 and the Nobel Prize for Literature in 1954.
While travelling back and forth between the United States, Europe, the Caribbean and Africa, Hemingway had a lifelong fascination for hunting and fishing and was shaped by the experience of war, aspects which make up major themes and settings of his stories. He was married four times; later in life he increasingly suffered from alcoholism and depression. On July 2, 1961, Ernest Hemingway committed suicide in his home in Ketchum, Idaho.
The short story "A Clean, Well-Lighted Place", a true classic of the genre which garnered particular praise from James Joyce, was first published in *Scribner's Magazine* in 1933 and included in the collection *Winner Take Nothing* of the same year.

F. Scott Fitzgerald (1896 – 1940)

Francis Scott Key Fitzgerald was born on September 24, 1896, in St. Paul, Minnesota. A literary talent at a young age, Fitzgerald attended Princeton University. However, he dropped out to join the American Army in 1917, at which time he met his future wife Zelda Sayre. After his discharge Fitzgerald moved to New York.

His first novel, *This Side of Paradise* (1920), became an immediate bestseller, which gave the newly-wed couple celebrity status. Their daughter Frances Scottie was born in 1921; three years later the Fitzgeralds moved to France, meeting with other expatriate American writers such as Ernest Hemingway and Gertrude Stein in Paris. The 1920s marked the decade which propelled Fitzgerald to literary fame. He published his novels *The Beauty and the Damned* (1922) and *The Great Gatsby* (1925) while writing countless short stories which he sold to magazines. Mainly for financial reasons Fitzgerald also worked for the Hollywood film industry. In the 1930s his marriage deteriorated due to Zelda's mental illness and his own abuse of alcohol. On December 21, 1940, F. Scott Fitzgerald died of a heart attack in Hollywood, California.

Fitzgerald is most famous for his novel *The Great Gatsby*, which has seen a number of film and other adaptations and continues to be read by generations of students. He is considered the foremost literary chronicler of the Roaring Twenties. Many of his works explore the era's affluent lifestyle. F. Scott Fitzgerald's literary themes include material wealth, glamour and troubled relationships. The short story "Babylon Revisited" was first published in 1931 in the *Saturday Evening Post*. It was reprinted in the posthumous collection *Babylon Revisited and Other Stories* (1960) and in *The Norton Anthology of American Literature*, 8th ed. (2013).

Langston Hughes (1902 – 1967)

James Mercer Langston Hughes was born on February 1, 1902, in Joplin, Missouri. He grew up in Cleveland, Ohio, and first took to writing poetry, publishing "The Negro Speaks of Rivers" in the African-American magazine *The Crisis* in 1921; it was included in his first poetry collection *The Weary Blues* (1926) and would later be considered his signature poem. After moving to Harlem, New York's neighbourhood of black counter-culture, Hughes briefly attended Columbia University; he earned a B. A. degree from Lincoln University, Pennsylvania, in 1929. In 1930 Hughes published his first novel *Not Without Laughter*, a commercial success, followed by his first short story collection *The Ways of White Folks* (1934). While living in Harlem he collaborated with writers like Zora Neale Hurston and became a key figure in the Harlem Renaissance, a cultural movement which explored African-American identity in various art forms. Hughes remained a highly prolific author throughout his life, publishing numerous collections of poetry, plays, critical essays and children's books. He also held academic teaching positions in creative writing programs. Langston Hughes died on May 22, 1967, in New York.

Hughes' texts often address racism and black identity, in particular the urban life of the working class; his poetry borrows from jazz, blues and spirituals.

"One Friday Morning" was first published in *The Crisis* in 1941 and later included in the collection *Laughing to Keep from Crying* (1952).

Leslie Marmon Silko (born 1948)

Being of Native American, white and Mexican descent, Leslie Marmon Silko was born on March 5, 1948, in Albuquerque, New Mexico. She grew up on the Laguna Pueblo reservation in west central New Mexico; on the one hand, she was exposed to tribal culture, the Keresan language and traditional storytelling as a young girl, while on the other hand, she attended a Catholic school in Albuquerque. In 1969 she earned a B. A. degree from the University of New Mexico. She published her first short story in the same year, the award-winning "The Man to Send Rain Clouds". Her first novel *Ceremony* (1977) received wide critical acclaim, telling the story of a traumatized veteran returning home from World War II. Among many other awards, Silko won a MacArthur Foundation "Genius Grant" in 1981, which allowed her to become a full-time writer and to quit her teaching positions. Also in that year, she published *Storyteller*, a collection of short stories, poems and photographs. Her later publications include essays, the novel *Almanac of the Dead* (1991) and the memoir *The Turquoise Ledge* (2010). Leslie Marmon Silko lives in Tucson, Arizona.

Silko's works highlight the contact zones between Native American life and contemporary American mainstream culture; she addresses, among other issues, her Laguna Pueblo heritage, tribal spirituality and the hardships Native Americans have to cope with in a predominantly white society. "Tony's Story" was published in *Storyteller* (1981) and reprinted in *The Scribner Anthology of Contemporary Short Fiction*, 2nd ed. (2007).

Jhumpa Lahiri (born 1967)

Nilanjana Sudeshna Lahiri was born on July 11, 1967, in London, England, to Bengali parents. At the age of two she immigrated with her family to Kingston, Rhode Island, where she started using her nickname "Jhumpa". In 1989 she received a B. A. from Barnard College before taking up graduate studies at Boston Univer-

sity, earning multiple Master degrees in Literature and a Ph. D. in Renaissance Studies. When Lahiri took to writing short stories, she at first had trouble placing them for publication. Nonetheless, her debut collection *Interpreter of Maladies* became an immediate commercial and critical success, winning a rare 'short-stories-only' Pulitzer Prize for Fiction in 2000. Lahiri's first novel *The Namesake*, published in 2003 and later adapted into a film, tells the story of a young Indian family settling in Cambridge, Massachusetts. Her second collection of short stories, *Unaccustomed Earth* (2008), peaked at number one in *The New York Times* bestseller list. In 2015 she was appointed professor of creative writing at Princeton University. Together with her husband and their two sons Jhumpa Lahiri has lived in Rome, Italy, since 2012. Many of Lahiri's stories centre on the immigrant experience of Indians in the United States. She explores the linguistic and religious gaps between the two cultures as well as generational gaps among immigrants. "Sexy" was first published in *The New Yorker* in 1998. The short story was included in *Interpreter of Maladies* (1999) and in *The Norton Anthology of American Literature*, 8th ed. (2013).

Junot Díaz (born 1968)

Junot Díaz was born on December 31, 1968, in Santo Domingo, Dominican Republic. When he was five years old his family immigrated to the United States. Díaz grew up both in Santo Domingo and in Parlin, New Jersey; he attended Rutgers University and received a B. A. before entering Cornell University and obtaining a Master of Fine Arts degree. While a student, Díaz worked all kinds of jobs to earn a living prior to his profession as a writer. *Drown* (1996), his first collection of short stories, deals with a family's immigrant experience; several pieces are narrated by Yunior, a Dominican American teen, who serves as a narrator in subsequent stories, too. Díaz reached fame and won critical acclaim with the novel *The Brief Wondrous Life of Oscar Wao* (2007), which was awarded the Pulitzer Prize for Fiction. In 2012 he released his second collection of short stories entitled *This Is How You Lose Her*. Junot Díaz is the recipient of a 2013 MacArthur Foundation "Genius Grant"; he is a professor of creative writing at the Massachusetts Institute of Technology. Díaz's stories mirror the lives, challenges and struggles of Dominican immigrants in the United States. Trademark elements of his writing are the use of Spanish slang, a young adult male perspective and New Jersey settings. "Nilda" was published in *The New Yorker* in 1999. It was reprinted in *The Scribner Anthology of Contemporary Short Fiction*, 2nd ed. (2007) and in the collection *This Is How You Lose Her* (2012).

Deborah Eisenberg (born 1945)

Born to Jewish parents on November 20, 1945, in Winnetka, Illinois, Deborah Eisenberg grew up in a Chicago suburb before moving to New York in the late 1960s. She graduated from the renowned New School of Social Research in New York. While working as a waitress she met actor Wallace Shawn, with whom she has lived ever since. Deborah Eisenberg started writing and publishing fiction relatively late in life. Her first collection of short stories *Transactions in a Foreign Currency* was released in 1986. Three more collections have followed to date, including *Twilight of the Superheroes* (2006). Eisenberg taught at the University of Virginia from 1994 until 2011, when she joined the faculty of Columbia University's MFA program. Her awards include a 1987 Guggenheim Fellowship, a 2009 MacArthur Foundation "Genius Grant" and a 2015 PEN/Malamud Award for "excellence in the art of the short story".
Eisenberg's fiction addresses various aspects of contemporary American life. "Twilight of the Superheroes" was published as the title story of her 2006 collection and reprinted in *The Scribner Anthology of Contemporary Short Fiction*, 2nd ed. (2007).

Charles Baxter (born 1947)

Charles Baxter was born on May 13, 1947, in Minneapolis, Minnesota. He graduated from Macalester College in St. Paul; in 1974 he received a Ph. D. in English from New York State University at Buffalo. Starting out as a high school teacher, Baxter has taught creative writing at several universities, ending in a long-term position at the University of Minnesota. To date, Baxter has published five novels including *The Feast of Love* (2000), a story based on Shakespeare's *Midsummer Night's Dream*, which was nominated for the National Book Award and later adapted into a film. He has also written a large body of short stories. In addition, he has published collections of essays and poetry. Among Baxter's honours is an American Academy of Arts and Letters award.
Much of Baxter's writing resonates with the life and culture of his native Minnesota.
"Charity" was published in *Timothy McSweeney's Quarterly Concern* (2013) and included in *The Best American Short Stories 2014*. It is also part of the collection *There's Something I Want You to Do* (2015), in which the individual stories are interwoven by a common set of characters and motifs.

Joan Silber (born 1945)

Joan Silber was born on June 14, 1945, in Newark, New Jersey. After receiving a B. A. degree from Sarah Lawrence College she moved to New York and completed an M. A. program at New York University. Her first novel *Household Words*, published in 1981, won a PEN/Hemingway Award. Three novels have followed to date, the most recent being *The Size of the World* (2008). Silber is a versatile writer of short stories. Her collections *In My Other Life* (2000), *Ideas of Heaven* (2004) and *Fools* (2013) were met with critical acclaim. Among other prizes, she won a Guggenheim Fellowship and an award from the American Academy of Arts and Letters. Joan Silber lives on the Lower East Side of Manhattan and teaches creative writing at nearby Sarah Lawrence College. She is fond of travelling, in particular to destinations in Asia.

In her writing Silber chooses a variety of settings ranging all across the globe. Some of her stories capture particularly long spans of time. "About My Aunt" was published in *Tin House* in 2014 and included in *The Best American Short Stories 2015*.

This collection

The texts of this collection were gathered from the vast amount of American short stories published between 1930 and 2015. The collection takes into account classic authors like Hemingway and Fitzgerald as well as acclaimed contemporary authors. As is the case with any anthology, the collection claims to be somewhat representative of the genre, but in fact it is the result of curricular requirements and of the editor's choice. It is primarily addressed to young adult readers aged 15 to 19 who take classes of English at a German-language secondary school. The reader's level of English is supposed to range between intermediate and advanced. The nine selected short stories allow the reader to refer to the three general topics frequently taught in the English classroom: the **American Dream, ethnic diversity** and **global challenges**. At the same time, however, each short story speaks for itself as a work of art, serving as an example of a **literary text** which enhances the reader's imagination, perception and intercultural awareness.

Ernest Hemingway, "A Clean, Well-Lighted Place"
First published: 1933   Setting: Spain, after World War I

An old man sits in a café and refuses to leave while two waiters have a conversation. One of them starts to ponder on existential questions.

Suggested topics: faith and religion; the individual and society; Lost Generation

F. Scott Fitzgerald, "Babylon Revisited"
First published: 1931   Setting: Paris, after the 1929 stock market crash

Charlie, a formerly rich American, returns to Paris, trying to obtain custody of his daughter. Honoria grows up with her stepparents Lincoln and Marion, the sister of Charlie's late wife.

Suggested topics: the American Dream; families and relationships; economic crises

Langston Hughes, "One Friday Morning"
First published: 1941   Setting: unnamed city in the American Midwest

Nancy Lee, an African-American high school student, is told by her headmaster Miss O'Shay that she will receive a fine arts scholarship. Full of anticipation, Nancy Lee prepares a speech.

Suggested topics: the American Dream; history of African Americans; racism

Leslie Marmon Silko, "Tony's Story"
First published: 1981   Setting: Laguna Pueblo reservation, New Mexico

Back on his reservation, army veteran Leon is knocked down by a police officer. When Leon and his friend Tony drive around in their car, they are chased by the same police officer.

Suggested topics: ethnic diversity (Native Americans); racism; police brutality

Jhumpa Lahiri, "Sexy"
First published: 1998   Setting: Boston

Miranda, a young office worker, has an affair with Dev, a married man from Bengal. Meanwhile, Miranda is told a similar story by her colleague Laxmi.

Suggested topics: ethnic diversity (Indian Americans); immigration; families and relationships

Junot Díaz, "Nilda"
First published: 1999   Setting: New Jersey

In their teenage years Dominican Americans Nilda and Rafa have a relationship. Their story is told by Yunior, Rafa's brother.

Suggested topics: ethnic diversity (Hispanic Americans); immigration; coming of age

Deborah Eisenberg, "Twilight of the Superheroes"
First published: 2006   Setting: New York City, 2004

Nathaniel, a comic book artist, shares a Manhattan downtown apartment with a group of peers. At the same time his uncle Lucien is trapped in the memories of his late wife and her family history.

Suggested topics: 9/11; US interventionism; history of immigration; the professional world

Charles Baxter, "Charity"
First published: 2013   Setting: Minneapolis; Seattle

As Matty Quinn, a former aid worker, can no longer afford his medication, he turns to drug dealer Black Bird. When Matty disappears, his boyfriend Harry starts searching for him.

Suggested topics: international development aid; health care; homosexuality

Joan Silber, "About My Aunt"
First published: 2014   Setting: New York City, 2012

Reyna raises her son Oliver while her partner Boyd is in prison. When Hurricane Sandy hits New York, she and her aunt Kiki assist each other.

Suggested topics: families and relationships; intercultural experience (Turkey); natural disasters; climate change

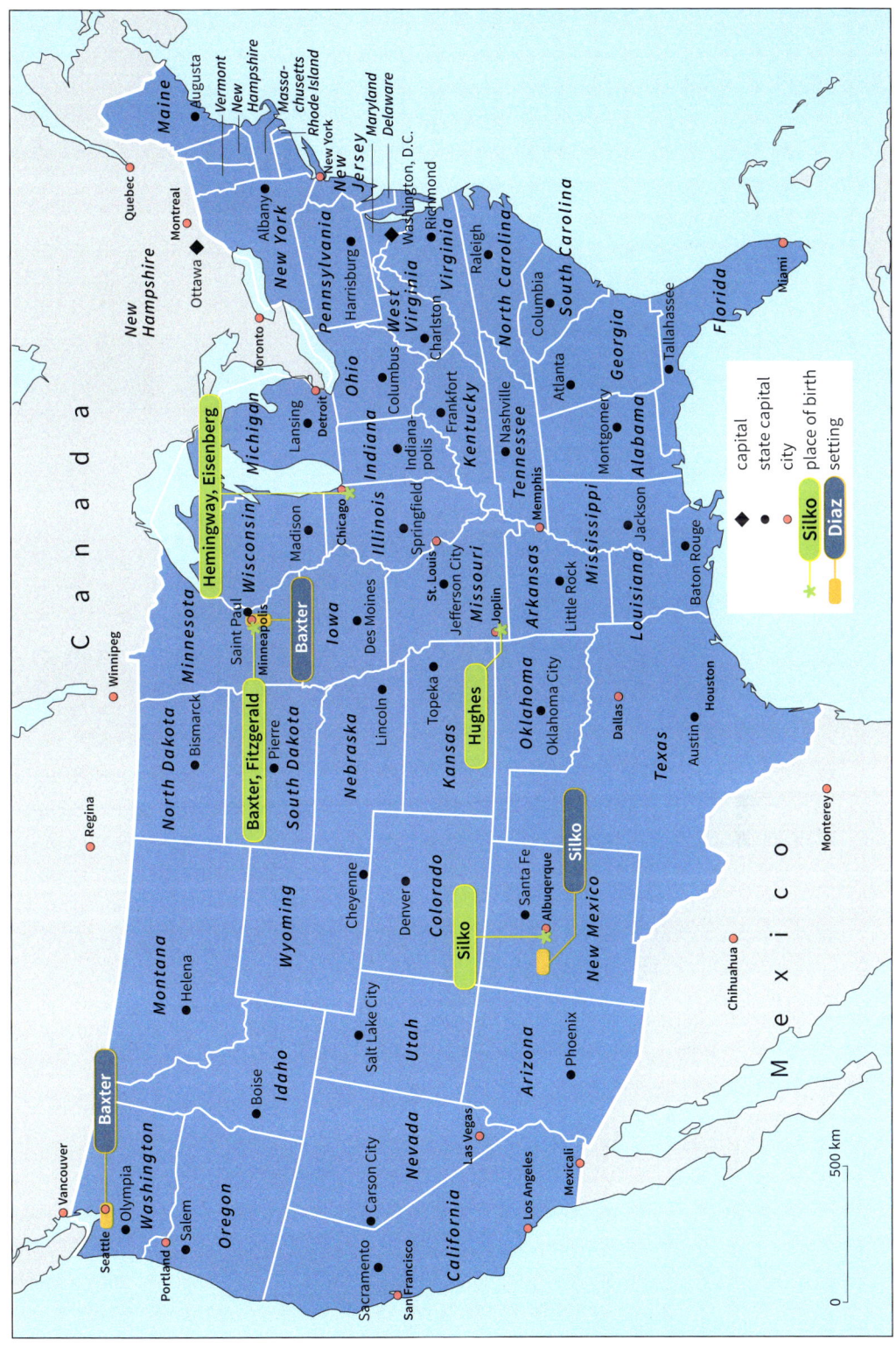

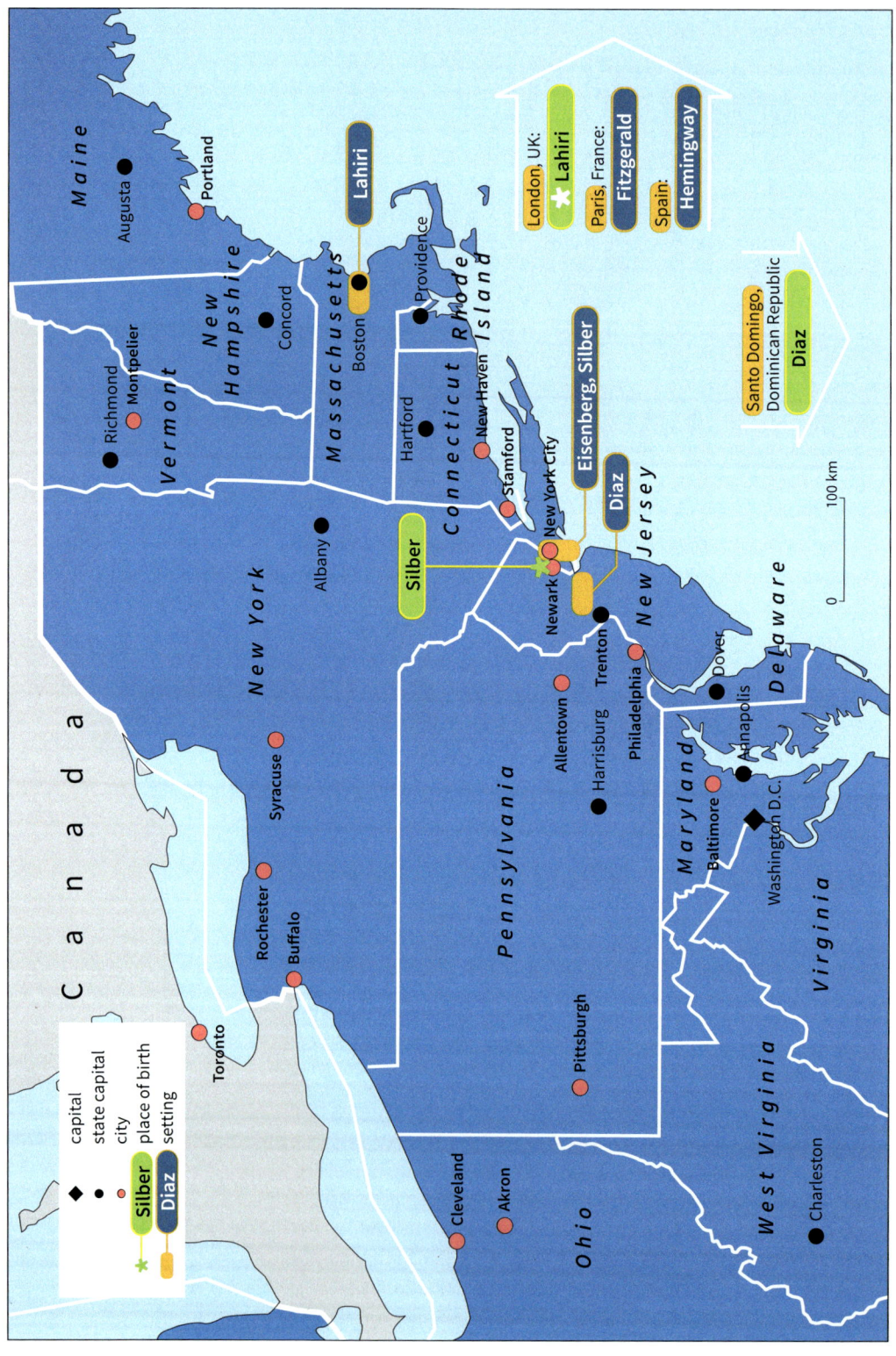

The American short story: Introduction to the genre and historical overview

In literary history the short story is a relatively new genre in its own right, originating, as many critics argue, in the United States in the early 19th century. However, as it relies on the universal art of storytelling, the short story is obviously linked to and developed from a number of predecessors: the anecdote, the fairy tale and the folk tale, and brief moralistic narratives like the parable and the fable. Despite many attempts the modern short story defies clear definition. It is almost impossible to find a valid set of characteristics, since the short story has proven to be a highly versatile form. Today, **any short piece of prose fiction** can be called a short story, if one adheres to a less dogmatic use of the term. In fact, countless authors and publishers, in particular those of the English language, have used the label for multiple forms of short narratives. Regardless of such variety most critics agree that short stories display narrative techniques of **reduction and compression**, i. e. short stories reduce or compress the basic component elements they share with novels: characters, plot and setting. What seems to set narrative genres apart, then, is length; but even here it is not feasible to define genre boundaries, as one can find novels of various length and novellas next to fairly long, multi-chapter short stories and short short stories. To be sure, the short story enables authors to employ **a great variety of structure, themes, narrative technique and length**.

Although it has been a popular form in many languages and literatures, the short story has a particularly strong tradition in United States. Indeed, the first examples of the genre as we understand it today are Washington Irving's "Rip Van Winkle" and "The Legend of Sleepy Hollow", published in 1820. Irving's short stories, together with those of Edgar Allen Poe and Nathaniel Hawthorne, are no longer the moralizing or didactic tales of previous generations; instead, these writers for the first time demonstrate that short fiction can be a suitable means to address **social and political concerns**, to explore **regional identity** and to examine the **human condition**. What added to the popularization and acceptance of the short story in America was a dynamic print market. By the middle of the 19th century, magazines like *The Atlantic Monthly* and *Harper's Magazine* started publishing short stories on a regular basis; the first book collections followed thereafter. Thus, as good short stories guaranteed readership and sales, ever more writers took to the new form. In the course of the 20th century, the short story developed into a well-established literary genre of considerable international reputation. It saw further artistic refinement as it allowed authors to draw on a wide range of subject matter and to test the limits of plot, temporal structure and narrative technique. Today, in the beginning of the 21st century, the American short story can be attributed many qualities: it is vibrant and elusive, artistic and entertaining, comic and tragic, realistic and fantastic, local and global, professionalized and competitive. Every year hundreds of short stories are published in magazines like *The New Yorker, Granta, Tin House, Five Points, Zoetrope* and *The Paris Review*, to name just a few. Annually edited collections like *The O. Henry Prize Stories* and *The Best American Short Stories* add to the list.

Significant authors of short stories outside the United States are, among many others, Rudyard Kipling, Guy de Maupassant, Anton Chekhov, James Joyce, Virginia Woolf, Albert Camus, Italo Calvino, Jorge Luis Borges, Gabriel García Márquez and Kenzaburō Ōe; acclaimed German language authors include Wolfgang Borchert, Heinrich Böll, Marie Luise Kaschnitz, Ilse Aichinger, Peter Bichsel and Ingo Schulze. Apart from the ones presented in this collection, many other American authors like Charlotte Perkins Gilman, Mark Twain, Stephen Crane, Sherwood Anderson, William Faulkner, John Steinbeck, Saul Bellow, Flannery O'Connor, James Baldwin, John Cheever, Raymond Carver, Sandra Cisneros, Amy Tan and T. C. Boyle are considered masters of the genre. In 2013 Canadian author Alice Munro won the Nobel Prize in Literature. It was for the first time that the prize was awarded solely on the basis of outstanding short stories.

Quotations from authors
1. Edgar Allen Poe (1809–1849)

We need only here say, upon this topic, that, in almost all classes of composition, the unity of effect or impression is a point of the greatest importance. It is clear, moreover, that this unity cannot be thoroughly preserved in productions whose perusal cannot be completed at one sitting. […] And, without unity of impression, the deepest effects cannot be brought about. Epics were the offspring of an imperfect sense of Art, and their reign is no more. […] Extreme brevity will degenerate into epigrammatism; but the sin of extreme length is even more unpardonable. In medio tutissimus ibis.

from: "Twice-Told Tales: A Review", *Graham's Magazine* (May 1842)

perusal reading

epigrammatism Epigrams are very short poems which can be witty or sarcastic. Example: "Little strokes fell great oaks." (Benjamin Franklin)
in medio tutissimus ibis (Latin) You will be safest taking the middle course.

2. Ernest Hemingway (1899–1961)

If a writer of prose knows enough of what he is writing about he may omit things that he knows and the reader, if the writer is writing truly enough, will have a feeling of those things as strongly as though the writer had stated them. The dignity of movement of an ice-berg is due to only one-eighth of it being above water. A writer who omits things because he does not know them only makes hollow places in his writing.

from: *Death in the Afternoon* (1932), chapter 16

to omit to leave out

3. Raymond Carver (1938–1988)

It's possible, in a poem or in a short story, to write about commonplace things and objects using commonplace but precise language, and to endow those things – a chair, a window curtain, a fork, a stone, a woman's earrings – with immense, even startling power. It is possible to write a line of seemingly innocuous dialogue and have it send a chill along the reader's spine.

from: "A Storyteller's Shoptalk", *The New York Times* (February 15, 1981)

innocuous harmless, seeming unlikely to provoke strong emotion

4. Jennifer Egan (born 1962)

I don't care very much about genre, either as a reader or as a writer. To me, fiction writing at any length, in any form, is a feat of radical compression: take the sprawling chaos of human experience, run it through the sieve of perception, and distill it into something comparatively miniscule that somehow, miraculous-

feat act of great skill or imagination

ly, illuminates the vast complexity around it. I don't think about short stories any differently than I do about novels or novellas or even memoirs. But the smaller scale of a story is important; the distillation must be even more extreme in order to succeed. It
⁵ also must be purer; there is almost no room for mistakes.

from: "Introduction", The Best American Short Stories 2014

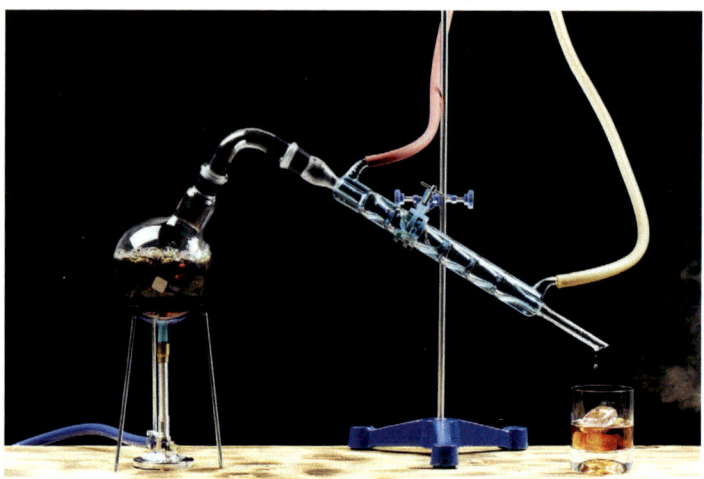

Developing skills

Contents:
1. Genre: Short story
2. Analysing fictional texts: Basic literary terms and definitions
3. Narrator and point of view: Useful expressions
4. How to write a characterization

1. Genre: Short story

- a type of prose fiction which usually deals with only a few characters
- rather short and less complex than a novel
- the title may hint at what the writer wants to point out
- presents characters at an important point in their lives
- is like a snapshot of a significant moment
- the number of characters, settings and events is limited
- the plot often covers one main incident; there is no subplot
- tends to begin **in medias res** (i. e. in the midst of action) and may have an **open** or a **surprise ending**
- various figures of speech help to emphasize the theme/message/author's intention (symbol, allusion, simile, metaphor, hyperbole, irony, etc.)
- …

2. Analysing fictional texts: Basic literary terms and definitions

Setting:
- the time and place of the events narrated in a story
- may include references to a historical period, time of day, season, weather conditions, social class, spatial surroundings and geographical locations
- creates a certain mood and atmosphere

Plot:
- the totality of events in a story
- includes the sequence of events, the emphasis they are given and the logical connection among them

- Freytag's dramatic structure of plot (only partly realized in short stories, if at all):
  → **exposition:** characters and setting are introduced
  → **rising action:** conflict is revealed, tension rises
  → **climax:** highest point of suspense, decisive point for further developments
  → **falling action:** complications begin to resolve
  → **denouement:** final outcome of events, solution of conflict

Character:
- a person who acts, appears or is referred to in a literary work
- can be either purely fictional or modelled on a historical person
- a **major character** is central to the story, while a **minor character** is rather marginal
- **protagonist:** the main character in a story, sometimes opposed by an **antagonist**
- a **round character** is complex, showing a variety of character traits, while a **flat character** is relatively simple, showing only a few character traits
- a **dynamic character** changes in the course of the story, while a **static character** does not

Narrator:
- the imaginary person who tells a story
  → the narrator assumes the voice of a **first-person** or a **third-person** speaker (or, less frequently, of a **second-person** speaker)
- the narrator and the author are not identical
  → a **reliable narrator** sticks to facts and is trustworthy, while an **unreliable narrator** gives false hints and is not consistent in his judgements and observations
  → an **intrusive narrator** addresses the reader directly and gives comments

Point of view:
- the perspective of the narrator
- point of view may shift or vary within one story

omniscient point of view
the narrator reveals the thoughts and feelings of multiple characters and/or knows everything relevant about the plot

objective point of view
the narrator is an uninvolved observer, having no access to the characters' thoughts and feelings

narrator
(first-person)
(second-person)
(third-person)

limited point of view
the narrator identifies with one character, revealing only this character's perception, thoughts and feelings

3. Narrator and point of view: Useful expressions

The author makes use of
- a first-person/third-person narrator
- a reliable/an unreliable/an intrusive narrator
- a narrator with a limited/an objective/an omniscient point of view

The narrator
- adopts a mixture of several points of view
- employs a shifting point of view
- presents the events from the outside
- functions as a camera-eye
- describes objectively/in great detail
- judges the characters
- comments on the behaviour/the appearance of the characters
- reflects on the situation/the political circumstances/the central conflict
- shares her thoughts/feelings/knowledge with the reader
- uses direct speech/indirect speech

The first-person narrator
- is the protagonist/a major character/a minor character in the story
- is limited in her point of view to what she experiences herself
- addresses the reader directly
- seems unreliable because he conceals information/contradicts himself
- uses interior monologue/stream of consciousness
- tells the story in retrospection
- digresses/inserts another story

The third-person narrator
- confines himself to the perception/experience/thoughts of a single character
- changes/varies/shifts her point of view
- is placed at the edge/takes the position of a neutral observer
- sticks to/disrupts the chronological order of events
- uses flashbacks/memories
- has access to the thoughts and feelings of more than one character
- shares his knowledge with the reader from an omniscient point of view

4. How to write a characterization

a) Mark/collect all the information that is given on a character.
b) Introduce the character and the situation he or she is in. Refer to the person's social background/position/job/role in the family.
c) Start characterizing him or her directly, i. e. state the age and sex, describe the person's outward appearance (hair, face, clothes, etc.), consider what is said directly about them – either by themselves or by others.
d) Refer to the traits of character that are revealed indirectly. Consider what a character does, how she or he reacts or behaves, what the person thinks and feels, what mood they are in, how they respond/communicate/interact with others.
e) Remember to refer to particular lines in the text in order to prove what you point out. Arrange different aspects in separate paragraphs. Clearly distinguish between the introduction, main part and conclusion.
f) Try to sum up if a character develops/changes in the course of events (→ round/dynamic character) or does not change his or her attitude (→ flat/static character).

Useful words and phrases
- X/Y is a man/woman in his/her fifties/thirties/…
- She is presented/described as …
- It is said that he looks/seems to be…
- On the one hand, he is portrayed/depicted as a person who …
- It is characteristic/typical of her that she behaves …/stays calm when …
- On the other hand, she reveals …
- He is also characterized by his attitude towards/reaction to …, which is revealed/underlined by his words/reactions/gestures/facial expression.
- She behaves aggressively/arrogantly/She pretends to be superior when…
- She speaks in a low/loud voice/shouts at …
- His emotions/feelings show that he is moved/nervous/excited/annoyed/irritated/confused/…
- She seems to feel insecure/convinced of herself/in a bad mood when she refers to/answers…
- This idea is revealed when he says that "…" (p. …, l. …).
- She is aware of the fact that …
- His behaviour shows that he is curious/jealous/frightened/taken by surprise/self-confident/convinced that…/interested in …
- Her way of treating X is harsh/friendly/gentle/arrogant/patronizing/contemptuous/aggressive/curious/…
- He creates the impression that he is a man who …
- An essential component of her character is her tendency to …
- The reader may conclude from her behaviour that …
- During the evening/the events that follow/In the course of action he undergoes a certain development/remains essentially unchanged, which proves that he is a round/flat character.
- The character changes her attitude towards …
- He is a flat/round character/an individual and not just a mere type.
- One can easily identify with him/You feel pity/sympathize with/dislike him because …
- Readers may ask themselves what they would do if they were in that situation/what they would have done if they had been in that situation/how they would have solved the problem/conflict.

Acknowledgements

Texts

pp. 6–9: "A Clean, Well-Lighted Place" by Ernest Hemingway (1933). Reprinted with the permission of Scribner, a division of Simon & Schuster, Inc. from WINNER TAKE NOTHING by Ernest Hemingway. Copyright © 1933 by Charles Scribners Sons. Copyright renewed 1961 by Mary Hemingway. All rights reserved.; pp. 29–36: "One Friday Morning" from SHORT STORIES by Langston Hughes. Copyright © 1996 by Ramona Bass and Arnold Rampersad. Reprinted by permission of Hill and Wang, a division of Farrar, Straus and Giroux.; pp. 37–42: Tony's Story' from STORYTELLER by Leslie Marmon Silko. Copyright © Leslie Marmon Silko 1981, used by permission of The Wylie Agency (UK) Limited.; pp. 43–62: "Sexy" from INTERPRETER OF MALADIES by Jhumpa Lahiri. Copyright © 1999 by Ihumpa Lahiri. Reprinted by permission of Houghton Mifflin Harcourt Publishing Company. All rights reserved.; pp. 63–70: "Nilda", from THIS IS HOW YOU LOSE HER by Junot Diaz, copyright © 2012 by Junot Diaz. Used by permission of Riverhead, an imprint of Penguin Publishing Group, a division of Penguin Random House LLC.; pp. 71–97: "Twilight of the Superheroes" from TWILIGHT OF THE SUPERHEROES by Deborah Eisenberg. Copyright © 2006 by Deborah Eisenberg. Reprinted by permission of Farrar, Straus and Giroux.; p. 98–110: Baxter, Charles: "Charity" from There's Something I Want You To Do: Stories (Pantheon Books, a division of Random House, 2015.) Copyright© 2013, 2015 by Charles Baxter. Originally appeared in McSweeney's Issue 43. Reprinted with permission. All rights reserved.; pp. 111–126: "About my Aunt" by Joan Silber. First published in Tin House, vol. 15, no. 4. Copyright © 2014 by Joan Silber. Reprinted by permission of Joan Silber. Reprinted by permission of Writers House LLC acting as agent for the author.

Pictures

|akg-images GmbH, Berlin: 127. |Alamy Stock Photo (RMB), Abingdon/Oxfordshire: Granger Historical Picture Archive 128. |Domke, Franz-Josef, Hannover: 135, 136. |Don Usner, Santa Fe: 129. |fotolia.com, New York: vadim_petrakov 139. |iStockphoto.com, Calgary: Lebazele 140. |MacArthur Foundation, Chicago: © John D. & Catherine T. MacArthur Foundation 131. |Marlborough Gallary, Inc., New York: © Richard Estes, courtesy Marlborough Gallery, New York 4, 4. |Pickett Pictures LLC, Minneapolis, MN 55414-1005: © 2010 Keri Pickett 131. |Picture-Alliance GmbH, Frankfurt a.M.: dpa/Garcia, Alejandro 130; dpa/Sachs, Ron 129. |Sarah Lawrence College, Bronxville, NY 10708: © Joan Silber 132. |ullstein bild, Berlin: Röhnert 127.